MW01609664

A Mother's Faith Journey
in the Face of Loss

**A Mother's Faith Journey
in the Face of Loss**

Laura
Leavens

SPECIAL
Copyright © 2015 by Laura Leavens

Printed in Canada

ISBN: 978-1-4866-0778-5

Word Alive Press
131 Cordite Road, Winnipeg, MB R3W 1S1
www.wordalivepress.ca

MIX
Paper from
responsible sources
FSC® C016245

Library and Archives Canada Cataloguing in Publication

Leavens, Laura, 1956-, author
        Special : a mother's faith journey in the face of loss / Laura Leavens.

Issued in print and electronic formats.
ISBN 978-1-4866-0778-5 (pbk.).--ISBN 978-1-4866-0779-2 (pdf).--
ISBN 978-1-4866-0780-8 (html).--ISBN 978-1-4866-0781-5 (epub)

        1. Leavens, Laura, 1956- --Family. 2. Vickery Hampson, Leiah, 1983-1998--Death and burial. 3. Children--Death--Religious aspects--Christianity. 4. Bereavement--Religious aspects--Christianity. 5. Mothers--Religious life. I. Title.

BV4907.L42 2015   248.8'66   C2015-902562-1
                                           C2015-902563-X

For Leiah

Each of us is unique; not all are special.

table of contents

acknowledgements

Thank you to all those who sowed a seed for this book and watered it along the way. It might have been a spoken word, a smile, a tear, a touch or an act of service. Your name may not be written on this page but your contribution was essential.

To my editor, Susan Fish, who shared this wisdom: "It takes two people to write a book: one to write it and one to tell her when it's done." Thank you for nudging me and for your excellent editing. To the many friends and supporters of Leiah and me, notably Anne and Ken Armstrong, Reverend Debbie Dennis, Sharon Ford (née Van Doodewaard), Lynn and Norm Gauthier, Desiree and Norman Torrie. To my family, in all its extended permutations, past and present. To my church family at Trinity Streetsville, notably those in my small groups, the prayer group, Stephen Ministry, and the Streetsville Coping Program. To members of Community Bible Study International, past and present, for walking the talk. To the scores of people who visited, wrote, called and prayed while

Leiah was in hospital and afterwards. To Bereaved Families of Ontario/Halton-Peel for being a life preserver and a means to give back. I also acknowledge all those who shared their deepest pain in my presence in a courageous effort to "help the healing begin." To the Brampton and Streetsville writers groups, for listening and nudging me to answer two questions, "Who are you writing this for? Is what you've written necessary for the story?" To Leiah's Daddy, Drew, and Dad, David, who helped make Leiah special. To Torey and Evann, simply for being Torey and Evann. To Michael, the companion, encourager and cook I dared to dream of. And to the One who sometimes calls us to do the impossible, yet promises to be with us always, in all ways. Thank you, God, for the gift of faith, the story of Abraham and Isaac, and the presence of family and friends who walk alongside us on dark, treacherous paths. And thank You, Father, for sacrificing your one and only Son to be our hope for future glory with you. May the story of this special girl touch hearts and draw them to the Way, the Truth and the Life. Amen.

foreword

This is a remarkable book, one that can be pointed to as significant and then returned to again and again. It is deeply moving and beautifully honest. Reading the manuscript reminded me of this family's time at the Hospital for Sick Children, a time I was given the opportunity to walk through with them. This hospital has been part of many stories, but this story offers its own unique thread in a fine fabric woven by the Creator to deepen our knowledge, understanding, wisdom and love.

This book has wisdom to offer to anyone who knows someone who has been through the loss of a loved one, particularly a child. The lessons about grief at the end are particularly useful.

Each of the lessons is learned through a set of circumstances that are reminiscent of the content of nightmares and our worst possible imaginings. How we respond to these events is the challenge that we as members of a community face. Our response is vital to our ability to bring healing to society.

As you read the book you are given a chance to see how one mother lives through the loss of her firstborn child and how, by reflecting on this experience and by naming the path through the depth of her grief, brings a light of knowing to herself. Laura moves beyond the telling of a series of sad and difficult events to a place of love and life. She shows us her encounter with doubts, anger, regrets and joys as she searches to find her daughter's legacy and to share it with us. A reading of *Special* may (and I hope will) give the reader strength and an understanding that in sharing even sad circumstances, we can bring joy and deeper blessings to our lives.

The loss of a child touches every possible experience that life has to offer—from the depths of despair to the heights of love and the breadth of human thought and feeling. Through this experience, this family (and Laura in particular) is brought an appreciation of the boundless potential that life offers and its sometimes terrible cost. The story of Leiah's life and death engages us with the delights and doubts of the human struggle. The wrestle to seek meaning, choose wisely, and live well are all here. The experience Laura describes brings to mind the story of Jacob and his own wrestle with a divine presence. Jacob, who is not a pillar of virtue in God's redemption history (who of us is?), comes to embrace a steadfast almost obstinate faith in God. Perhaps faith is obstinate, but by persevering Laura, like Jacob, is made more deeply aware of the Creator's blessing.

I am grateful to Laura and her families for sharing their story and am particularly grateful for the life of Leiah Vickery Hampson and all she continues to mean.

Michael Marshall, Chaplain
March 5, 2015

introduction

Special is the story of a girl—my daughter, Leiah—who was stricken with a sudden and unexpected illness at the age of fourteen. Feeling special was of great importance to Leiah, but she also made a lot of people feel special.

The Merriam-Webster Dictionary says that *special* means: distinguished by some unusual quality; especially: being in some way superior (our special blend); held in particular esteem (a special friend); readily distinguishable from others of the same category: unique (they set it apart as a special day of thanksgiving); of, relating to, or constituting a species: specific; being other than the usual: additional, extra; designed for a particular purpose or occasion.

On these pages, these definitions come to life. The words that follow are mostly mine, but some are Leiah's and others come from family and friends who glimpsed her from different vantage points. Many of the reminiscences and hard-won insights come from the pages of a diary I kept during Leiah's illness as well as one I penned around the time of her birth.

This story hinges on the story of another special child. When Leiah was sick, family friends came to visit and Des prayed with me. Later, her husband Norm said that he had seen angels and had received a word from God to share a Bible story with me. It's one of those stories that makes us squirm: the story of God asking Abraham to take his long-awaited, special son, Isaac, to a mountain in Moriah to sacrifice him on an altar. Here's the story:

Sometime later God tested Abraham. He said to him, "Abraham!" "Here I am," he replied. Then God said, "Take your son, your only son, whom you love—Isaac—and go to the region of Moriah. Sacrifice him there as a burnt offering on a mountain I will show you." Early the next morning Abraham got up and loaded his donkey. He took with him two of his servants and his son Isaac. When he had cut enough wood for the burnt offering, he set out for the place God had told him about. On the third day Abraham looked up and saw the place in the distance. He said to his servants, "Stay here with the donkey while I and the boy go over there. We will worship and then we will come back to you." Abraham took the wood for the burnt offering and placed it on his son Isaac, and he himself carried the fire and the knife. As the two of them went on together, Isaac spoke up and said to his father Abraham, "Father?" "Yes, my son?" Abraham replied. "The fire and wood are here," Isaac said, "but where is the lamb for the burnt offering?" Abraham answered, "God himself will provide the lamb for the burnt offering, my son." And the two of them went on together. When they reached the place God had told him about, Abraham built an altar there and arranged the wood on it. He bound his son Isaac and laid him on the altar, on top of the wood. Then he reached out his hand and took the knife to slay his son. But the angel of the Lord called out to him from heaven, "Abraham! Abraham!" "Here I am," he replied. "Do not lay a hand on the boy," he said. "Do not do anything to him. Now I know that you fear God, because you have not withheld from me your son, your only son."Abraham looked up and there in a thicket he saw a ram caught by its horns. He went over and took the ram and sacrificed it as a burnt offering instead of his son. So Abraham called that place The Lord Will Provide. And to this day it is said, "On the mountain of the Lord it will be provided." The angel of the Lord called to Abraham from heaven a second time and said, "I swear by myself, declares the Lord, that because you have done this and have not withheld your son, your only son, I will surely bless you and make your descendants as numerous as the stars in the sky and as the sand on the seashore. Your descendants will take possession of the cities of their enemies, and through your offspring all nations on earth will be blessed, because you have obeyed me." (Genesis 22:1-18)

Des told me that God was quite clear: just as Abraham had, I was supposed to hand Leiah over to God and entrust Him with her care.

I was shocked. I didn't want to give Leiah to God. Unprepared to let her go, I couldn't imagine severing the cord that connected me to her, and living in a world without my daughter. She'd been there every day for the past fourteen-and-a-half years. For her not to be there? Impossible! But then I reasoned that it had worked out well for Abraham and Isaac. God had provided a sacrifice—the ram—and Abraham had been able to keep Isaac.

Like Abraham's experience on Mount Moriah, this story is about a test—a really big one.

I borrowed phrases from the well-known poem *Monday's Child* for chapter titles of this book because this is a story about several long weeks of days. Some were full of grace, others full of woe, and many were just plain hard. Eerily, Wednesdays were often *woeful* precursors of *far-to-go* Thursdays, while Fridays (and one in particular) tested the limits of *loving and giving*. Words from a sermon given by Reverend Kyle Hackmann in the spring of 2014 captured the essence of *that* Friday:

> When you lose everything you need most, and it feels like God is calling you into the unknown, trust Him. He pushes you to the point where you won't give him what you hold back, but He wants your *everything* and is willing to test you to get it.

> *Monday's Child is fair of face*
> *Tuesday's Child is full of grace*
> *Wednesday's Child is full of woe*
> *Thursday's Child has far to go*
> *Friday's Child is loving and giving*
> *Saturday's Child works hard for a living*
> *And a child that's born on the Sabbath Day*
> *Is bonny and blithe and good and gay.*
> -First recorded in E. Bray's Traditions of Devonshire

Part 1
before

Wednesday

woe

After six weeks in a drug-induced coma, Leiah was not getting better. The swelling in her brain would not come down and the seizures continued. Her doctors called a meeting.

The plan was to take her off life support on Thursday. She would either breathe on her own—or not. I searched my soul, and what I could glean of my fourteen-year-old daughter's. Although I wanted to hang on to Leiah any way I could, it wasn't my choice. It was hers. I racked my brain for anything she might have said about a situation like this, but nothing came to mind. As I paused, an image of my freckle-faced, spirited child came to mind. *That* child would not want to be tied to life artificially. Heaviness filled me as I realized what I had to do. Slowly, solemnly and wordlessly, I nodded my assent to the plan.

Even so, I was not ready to let her go.

I slept beside Leiah that Wednesday night. Careful to avoid the tangle of lines and tubes, I climbed into her hospital bed and snuggled beside her, trying to imprint her essence upon my memory. She became my silent confessor to unspoken emotions and regret.

Why had this happened? Why hadn't I realized how sick she was? How could I have been so blind to miss the clues? She had even told me.

***

It had been a Monday, six weeks earlier. Leiah had been home from school, sick with the flu. While she lay on the family room couch, I puttered in the kitchen. Mid-sweep I heard her call "Mom?" I stopped my task and went to her. Her face revealed nothing about what she was about to say. I assumed she wanted a drink of water or a snack. Instead she asked, "Mom, am I going to die?"

Where had that *question come from? Die? Of course not. She had the flu.* I started to rationalize. *She's just being over-dramatic. After all, she's a teenager...she's hormonal...yet, she must be feeling really cruddy to ask such a question.*

I answered softly, "Of course not, dear. You just haven't had a flu this bad before. You're used to perking up in a day or two. Remember what the school secretary said? There's a bad strain going around, one that lasts a week."

Seemingly satisfied with my response, Leiah returned her gaze to the television, and I went back to sweeping. I pondered her question a moment longer before dismissing it completely. *Of course she's not going to die. Fourteen-year-olds don't die.*

***

Lying beside my unmoving, unconscious child, regret threatened to swallow me whole. *If only I'd gone over to her that day...if only I'd looked into her eyes to see what was behind the question...if only I'd talked to my daughter while she could still speak...*

I started to cry silently as I nestled closer to her and whispered in her ear, "I'm so sorry, Leiah. I wish I'd…oh, I love you so much." I held on to her tightly and thought back to before this horrid illness had struck, a sickness that severed our lives into *Before* and *After*.

A Snapshot
of normal life

Ours was a busy family of five (six, if you count the dog) living in Mississauga, Ontario in the spring of 1998. Monday to Friday meant school for my husband, David (who was a teacher), and for our girls, Leiah, eight-year-old Torey and five-year-old Evann, while the dog and I stayed home. It was *de rigueur* for the dog but new for me.

After seventeen years in the work world—the last fourteen as a working mom—things had changed rather abruptly in September 1996. I'd gone to an after-work open house at a company in downtown Toronto. One moment I was standing confidently in my chocolate brown suit and matching pumps, nibbling on a yummy brownie; the next moment I was on the floor, unconscious. After a trip to Emergency at St. Michael's Hospital where doctors found no obvious physical cause, I was sent home with a prescription: "Don't go into work tomorrow and go see your family doctor."

It was the beginning of a seventeen-month journey of physical, mental and spiritual healing that came with perks. Perk #1: I didn't have to work. Perk #2: I had time to actually listen to my husband and kids instead of barking out orders and rushing past them. Perk #3: I recognized I was starved physically, mentally and spiritually.

Feeding the first need was easy: I started each day with a toasted cheddar cheese bagel dripping in butter. The second and third, somewhat intertwined, took more time and attention, requiring doctor's care supplemented by spiritual nourishment. Our local church, Trinity Streetsville, became my second home. No longer tied to job-related details, my mind was freed up for other things. Words from sermons and Scripture started to make sense and sink in; I revelled in all I was discovering.

I needed all the spiritual encouragement I could get. Even without work, life was hectic with three kids and an aging dog. At five pounds and with spunk that belied his age, our Maltese terrier Hammy was a senior in dog years. Scheduling vet visits around everything else—soccer games, piano lessons, AWANA (a Christian children's program), youth group and my activities—was daunting, especially since we gave up our second car when I stopped working. With the assistance of friends who carpooled, we managed.

Weekends were especially busy for Leiah. A teenager now, she had an active social life. Sometimes it was tough for her to decide between invitations from friends, and those from her two sets of families.

Leiah had been the only child from my first marriage. Drew and I had separated around the time of Leiah's birth. Leiah was three-and-a-half when I married David, and a few years older when Drew married Ann. Leiah called her father *Daddy,* and her stepfather, *Dad.* Many but not all weekends Leiah saw Drew and his family. Between David's and my burgeoning extended families there were plenty of birthdays and anniversaries to celebrate. Drew's side of the family was smaller but Leiah also joined Ann's family get-togethers—and as she was the only child, grandchild, great-grandchild and niece on her father's side, Leiah was the star of the family.

Leiah twinkled in David's and my family too. As the first female grandchild on David's side, and as the first grandchild, great-grandchild and niece on my side, she got a lot of attention. They all watched her grow from a chubby, bright-eyed baby into a sturdy, wilful toddler, and eventually a petite five-foot-two-inch young lady with lanky limbs, long, thick, slightly wavy medium-brown hair, and a great sense of humour. Her sparkling blue eyes set off a ready smile in a slender face dotted with freckles. A blend of personality types, Leiah was both introspective and social. She kept a diary for private thoughts, but thrived on being around people. A natural at some but not all sports, she jumped at opportunities to ski in the winter. The other three seasons were reserved for one of her major passions, Canada's Wonderland, a theme park north of Toronto. Leiah's friend Sharon recalls Wonderland visits:

"We had similar preferences with respect to roller coasters (the bigger and faster the better) so it worked well. We went one summer with Mr. Hampson, Evann and Torey. The deal was that Leiah and I were allowed to go around by ourselves while he took the girls. We were to meet at a particular restaurant by one. Leiah and I tried to maximize the number of rides we went on by strategically selecting ones that didn't have overly long line-ups, although we had a few mandatory roller coasters we wanted to ride. We ran all over the amusement park that morning trying to get to as many rides as possible and were quite proud of our progress when the time came to meet for lunch.

"We were both stunned when Mr. Hampson greeted us with a stern expression. As we got closer, he said, in an equally stern voice, 'You're an hour late!' We were astounded. I held up my wristwatch as proof that it was only one o'clock—that we weren't late—he must be mixed up. He looked at it, and pointed to the clock on the wall that clearly read five to two. We all realized what had happened—the battery in my watch had died. He said, 'Well it must have felt like an incredibly long morning to you guys!' Leiah and I breathed a sigh of relief that we weren't in too much trouble.

"The rest of the day was a lot of fun. We hit up a few more roller coasters and then went to the waterpark where we rode only the fastest waterslides. When it was time to go, I remember badly wishing we could stay, but Evann and Torey were quite young then, and I am sure they were tired out. It was a fun day, and one well worth remembering."

When she couldn't get a ride to Wonderland, Leiah chose shopping and movies as go-to activities. Our local mall afforded both options. Sharon remembers going to the movies to see Dante's Peak at the Erin Mills Town Centre. "In hindsight, the movie was totally far-fetched, but at the time we thought it was the most exciting film we had ever seen. What was fun about that experience—apart from the excitement of watching a live volcano on the brink of exploding for two hours—was the element of spontaneity in deciding to go to the movies at all. We were at the mall with some time and we chose that movie from among the shows that were playing. It made us feel grown up."

Leiah often sketched, painted and made crafts. David's mother, Ann Wray Hampson, known as Anna to her grandchildren, recalls Leiah's "love of crafts, making things with her hands, and how her eyes would sparkle in a craft store—or one that sold stickers, for that matter."

Combining an afternoon of craft-making with dishing over teen heartthrobs was a double delight. Sharon recalls reading *Bop* magazine when the girls were in grades 5 and 6 and obsessing over the hunks of the day—"Jonathan Taylor Thomas and Brandon something or other." She also remembers a period of time in junior high when fabric paints were popular. "One day, Leiah and I painted t-shirts, both using similar designs to create shirts that had big flower blossoms all across the front. I really cherished mine, as much for the great memory of making it as for the pride in my designs. I still might have that somewhere." She remembers when friendship bracelets were a big trend and how for her birthday that year Leiah gave her a case with different colours of thread and beads for making friendship bracelets. "I was struck by the generosity of the gift and really valued it—it considerably enhanced my output of friendship bracelets! I did not keep many of my childhood things but I did keep that case, with some of the thread still remaining…I believe I still have it somewhere too."

Leiah and Sharon laughed a lot, but shared a serious side. Sharon wanted to be a doctor when she grew up while Leiah planned to be an architect. Leiah's desire might have been borne out of a family habit: on weekends David and I often dragged the kids to model homes and returned with housing plans. Hours of poring over plans, comparing different-shaped rooms and designs might have piqued her interest in architecture. As a child and young teen, that interest translated into making model homes out of shoe boxes and larger containers. Anna remembers "the concentration Leiah brought to her labyrinthine 3-D housing constructions."

"I do not recall having any other friends at that relatively young age who shared in my dreams for the future the way Leiah did," says Sharon. "We had this vision in our minds—

Leiah being an architect, me a doctor, living in fancy condos in California with successful careers and picture-perfect lives. Much of it was undoubtedly inspired by the images of prime time television dramas, but these dreams were also rooted in an underlying ambition to accomplish something of significance in the future. I believe Leiah had the drive to pursue her dreams even at that age, as did I."

Leiah delighted in entertaining an audience, often directing and starring in home fashion shows. Friend and neighbour Anne Armstrong, whose daughter Victoria was a friend of Leiah's, remembers "how Leiah could mimic people's accents so well (especially one of the associate priests at church). She was always doing it! I remember so well the fashion shows they both put on for us and seeing these beautiful girls come downstairs in all their different attire! I just loved it so much! Leiah could be so zany and yet so demure. She was gentle, a real 'lady', and above all, she so loved Jesus."

***

Children were drawn to Leiah, and she to them. At 13, after studying hard, she passed a Babysitters' Training Course exam and proudly flashed her Canada Safety Council certificate before rushing up to her room to design flyers to advertise her services in the neighbourhood, to decorate a sturdy cardboard boot box, labelled "Leiah's Activitie Box" [sic], and to cram it with crayons, colouring books, *Owl* magazines, and storybooks. I can still picture her heading out purposefully for her first official job, her trusty box tucked under one arm. As a former Brownie and Girl Guide, Leiah had taken to heart their motto to "Be prepared."

Leiah's grandmother Anna remembers Leiah as a beacon to her younger cousins: "Leiah was the first granddaughter, second eldest grandchild, and had a unique role in this family.

Slight as she was, she was a kind of Pied Piper to the younger ones as they came along, often with a good-sized toddler on her hip and others clustering around her. They clearly felt safe with her, and loved to be with her. Her arrival at gatherings was always preceded by cries of 'Where's Leiah?' She was the kind of big sister anyone would wish for. She put down roots in our family, and the others took root around her. My daughter-in-law Anne [Hampson] remembers how patient, coaxing and reassuring Leiah was with Anne's daughter's Emma, helping her to get into the pool. Leiah was curious and observant and good to be with. She enlarged our lives."

Leiah's creative repertoire was extensive. She co-hosted in-house radio programs, wrote, directed and performed many songs and plays with friends, sisters and cousins. Yet those events paled in comparison with the focus she put into planning and executing her annual birthday party. Leiah simply *had* to celebrate the day she was born. Her birthday parties made her feel special—really special. Feeling special was of great importance to her.

Pre-party, Leiah was organizer extraordinaire. During an event, she transformed into Queen Bee, or, more accurately, Princess Leiah, holding court over her subjects and exuding a confidence that belied the niggling insecurities she struggled with at other times. Since Leiah was part of many families by virtue of remarriage, her celebrations carried on for weeks. After all, she had two sets of parents, several sets of grandparents, and a few great-grandparents, as well as aunts, uncles and cousins galore.

Being born in September posed a challenge for birthday party planning. The first day after Labour Day meant a new school year, and a different crop of classmates. Leiah wanted a mix of old and new friends at each year's birthday party, which meant there was no time to lose. On the first day of school each year, her mission was to scope out her class and rapidly assess which ones were friend-material. Names of the lucky few were added to her list of forever friends. Decisions had to be made promptly as invitations for an end-of-month party had to go out within a week of school starting.

After deciding on a party theme, locale and budget, it was time to send out invitations. When negotiations between Leiah and us took too long, she'd have to settle for store-bought cards. Otherwise, Leiah designed colourful, sparkly invitations for each person. During her toddler and low single-digit years there was a mix of home parties and forays to Chuck E. Cheese and McDonald's Playland. As she grew older, options diverged. Sharon remembers several of Leiah's birthdays:

"Leiah's birthdays were always exciting. The first birthday of Leiah's that I ever attended was a sleepover and it was a ton of fun. There were so many excited girls packed into the basement that sleeping bags lined the entire floor. I think we watched *The Nightmare Before Christmas*.

"The birthday party that stands out in my mind was at Erin Mills Town Centre. We started by playing a round of mini-golf at the course in the mall, and then went to JJ Muggs for dinner. It was *the* birthday party of the sixth grade. I think the birthday cake was chocolate with sparklers on it, though I couldn't say for sure. I remember it as a special day, and a big event in the life of an eleven- or twelve-year-old. I am inclined to think that was a particularly special birthday for Leiah too. There was something about the excitement of the girls in attendance and the way we felt all grown up sitting around together eating our meals and sipping our sodas—but that's me projecting my adult perspective on it. Maybe it was just plain fun.

"Leiah's fourteenth birthday stands out in my memory too. It was at her new house. At that time Leiah had started going to a different school for ninth grade, so there were some old familiar faces at the party as well as some new ones. We came over in the evening and I think we ate pizza for dinner and had cake afterwards. There were helium-filled balloons in the hall. We went to the upstairs bathroom, which was full of beauty products, including nail polish, makeup and hair products. I had recently developed some skill with a nail polish brush, and after painting Leiah's nails, I painted the nails of a few others.

"I slept over that night, and Leiah and I ate most of [the candy] while watching movies that night and the next morning. I specifically remember watching *Romeo and Juliet* (the one with Leonardo Di Caprio). We may have argued a little over who had the superior claim to marry him.

"I distinctly remember leaving the next day and experiencing the sensation of regret that the party was over. Maybe it was because Leiah was at a new school and I didn't see her as much, or maybe it was because we had such a great time—I just didn't want it to end.

"At some point during the party, a photograph was taken in the hallway by the balloons with all of the girls at the party. I kept that photograph for many years, always remembering the party and wishing there was a way to step back into that moment."

One

long tuesday

The time *before* our Wednesday of woe in the spring of 1998 could be seen as one long Tuesday—full of grace—although with a few hiccups.

In her final month as a thirteen-year-old, Leiah started grade nine at John Fraser Secondary School. It was a winning location for a teenage shopaholic: the school was across the street from a shopping mall. But there was a downside. Her friends were eight kilometres away at Meadowvale Secondary School.

We had moved out of our old neighbourhood when Leiah was partway through grade seven. She had not been happy about it. The day we told her someone had bought the house, Leiah camped out under the dining room table with bedding and books. Defiant, she spit out her words, "Fine. You can leave, but I'm staying. The new people will just have to accept me as a tenant." Eventually she relented, while drawing a line in the sand. "I *won't* change schools. I want to stay with my friends at Edenwood [her middle school]." After some negotiation, the Edenwood principal allowed her to complete grades seven and eight with her friends.

The choice to stay at Edenwood created issues. The school was three kilometres from our new home—not an insurmountable distance, but farther than she was used to walking. Neither a forty-minute walk, nor the same time by two buses, was appealing. Since David worked nearby he agreed to drive Leiah to school as long as she was ready to go when he was. The problem was that Leiah liked to sleep in. Most mornings were steeped in tension, culminating in David's voice booming, "Leiah, hurry up. I'm leaving *now!*" Leiah usually came down the stairs in the nick of time.

One morning the nick of time had passed. David announced he'd had enough of being almost late for work. I told him to leave, then summoned strength to deal with the fallout. Minutes later when Leiah descended the stairs to discover her taxi had departed, she was indignant. Mumbling about the unfairness of it all, and how *we'd* made her late, she dashed out the door half-sprinting up the street.

She was ready early the next day.

Leiah's grade eight graduation in June 1997 was a major transition. It meant cutting ties with friends she'd grown up with and leaving her old stomping grounds, to make new friends and start high school in a new area. But first, there was an important decision to make: what to wear to the graduation ceremony and dance. The search for the perfect ensemble began in earnest in April. Although I was initially grumpy about the fuss over a middle school graduation, I soon became caught up in Leiah's infectious excitement. Finding a dress was remarkably easy. Success was ours the first day. Within seconds of entering Suzy Shier on the lower level of Erin Mills Town Centre, we spotted a spaghetti-strapped long, slinky, navy blue sheath with cheerful, large, white and light blue daisies. Leiah's eyes lit up. My eyes lit up when I saw the price: twenty-five dollars.

"Try it on," I urged, handing her the hanger. When she emerged from the change room to check her reflection, we heard Leiah's name being called. It was Sharon! Both friends had chosen the same store at the same time to find their perfect graduation dress. Dark-haired five-foot-two Leiah stood beside blonde five-foot-ten Sharon, comparing each of their images in the mirror. Sharon's purple dress made her face light up, but needed lengthening to accommodate her height. Leiah's dress made her eyes sparkle, but dragged along the floor. Fortunately each dress could be altered. Both girls left the store beaming.

The quest for footwear was less speedy and not as kind to my budget. After weeks of scouring shoe stores in several malls, Leiah finally spotted a white-heeled sandal. She pulled it off the shelf and showed it to me. "I think this is it," she said smiling as she fingered the multiple straps. White matched the daisies on her dress and the three-inch heels made her feel grown up. The outfit was complete.

On graduation day, I took her to my hairdresser who curled and arranged Leiah's long locks into a soft up-do, leaving tendrils at each side to soften and frame her jawline. Leiah looked stunning but there was no time to linger. We had to hurry home for makeup, dressing and posing for photos on the front lawn.

Her father, Drew, arrived to drive his princess to the graduation ceremony, giving her the seat of honour up front. Mere maidservant cum photographer I was relegated to the backseat. Camera at the ready I called, "Hey, Leiah." She turned her head. *Click.* Never had she looked so gorgeous, her smile so captivating, her bearing so confident. It was a very special photo of a very special girl on a momentous day.

After the graduation ceremony Leiah and her friends posed for pictures in front of the school, before leaving to go inside for the dance. It was a bittersweet day for her—a time to celebrate her middle school graduation, while knowing she had to say goodbye to friends she'd seen almost daily for six years.

Three months later, in September 1997, Leiah started high school. As usual, her first job was assessing her new classmates for potential invitees to her fourteenth birthday party. It was harder this year, because she didn't know any of them. Deciding who might become new friends and mix well with her old friends took longer than usual, so her birthday party happened a little later that fall. She decided on a home party and invited a mix of old and new friends. A piñata hung from the rafters in the unfinished basement and everyone took a whack at it. It was a particularly sturdy paper animal, as partygoers got second, third and fourth chances before the piñata finally cracked open, spilling Cherry Blasters and assorted treats on to the floor. Little sisters Torey and Evann watched quietly from the stairs. When the scavenging mayhem began, the two of them slipped quietly in between the older kids to pick up any missed sweets on the floor.

When the party ended, everyone posed for a photo to mark the occasion.

Another successful party courtesy of "Birthdays by Leiah."

Life carried on, each week with its natural ebb and flow. Each day and night of the week was reserved for something specific: I went to a small group through church one night, Torey and Evann went to AWANA another evening, and Leiah went to youth group yet another night. Some nights were reserved for staying at home to watch favourite television shows, such as *Party of Five*, Leiah's favourite TV show, on Wednesday. Friday evening meant piano lessons for Leiah, followed by a trip to Domino's Pizza to pick up the "two medium pizza deal." Our standard order was one pizza with cheese and three toppings, and a cheeseless, meaty one with plenty of sauce for David. If a female family member wanted a third slice, she'd be forced to take a piece of David's cheeseless pizza. Torey started to prefer the cheeseless one, so numbers tended to work out.

Friday March 6, 1998 was a regular day except that Leiah came home from school feeling like she was coming down with something. Nevertheless she soldiered on, going to her piano lesson and home via Domino's where she dined on pizza with the rest of us.

On Saturday morning, one of Leiah's friends called suggesting a trip to the theatre to see *Titanic* for the fifth time. Normally Leiah would jump at a chance to see her onscreen crush, Leonardo DiCaprio. That day, however, Leiah declined the invitation and decided to stay in her room and sleep.

On Sunday, Leiah, Torey, Evann and I normally went to church where Leiah volunteered in *Sonshine Land*, the Sunday School class for preschoolers. She'd fallen into the job. Although Torey was content to go to Sunday School unaccompanied, Evann refused to go on her own. Her sister, Leiah, however, had the magic touch. Evann trusted her. Karen, a friend whose daughters are around the same ages as Torey and Evann, remembers the first time she met Leiah:

"Evann would not leave Leiah's side in the old Sunday School classroom in the old church—it was awesome to watch their interaction."

Mark North, who taught *Sonshine Land*, remembers:

"Evann would be shy at first, so Leiah would stay with her for the whole class. It wasn't long before Leiah offered to help and become an unofficial part of the team. One of the things I most admired about Leiah was how she presented herself as a very shy and unassuming girl, but underneath you could see there was strength. I didn't know Leiah on a personal level but I always had her pegged for a teacher later in life. She had a quiet and easy way with children and I think she enjoyed working with them. Leiah seemed to take the responsibility of assisting and teaching a lot more seriously than most of the youth that helped in Sunday School—that's not to knock the other kids, but when Leiah said she was going to be there to help, she was. And when she knew she couldn't help, she made the effort to let me know, something else I greatly respected her for. I can't tell you how helpful her assistance was. It allowed me to become better at teaching while she tended to some of the distractions. Whenever someone said to me, 'Oh, Leiah is the helper,' I would say, 'No! Leiah is the assistant teacher.' I came to the realization I had the ability and the will to teach kids from my years in *Sonshine Land,* and Leiah was one of the people that helped me to come to that realization."

If she could have, Leiah would have been in *Sonshine Land* on March 8, but she didn't feel well enough to go. She stayed home with her dad.

On Monday, David, Torey and Evann went off to school while Leiah and I stayed home. When I called the school to let them know she was sick, the secretary told me there was a bad strain of flu going around. Leiah's symptoms included a headache and warm forehead. I took her temperature. When the thermometer registered 39.5 degrees Celsius I gave her some Tylenol and poured a bubble bath. As she lay in the bath, Leiah asked, "Where am I?" I reminded her we were in the en suite bathroom, not the one she shared with her sisters.

After her bath I took her arm to help her downstairs to the family room couch so she could rest and watch television in comfort. I flitted in and out, between kitchen and laundry duties. It was that afternoon when she looked over at me and asked, "Mom, am I going to die?"

The next morning, Tuesday, Leiah still felt unwell. It was time to call the doctor. Leiah asked if she could see one of the female doctors in the practice. We'd had the same male family doctor since she was four, but now that she was a teenager, she preferred to speak to a woman. The receptionist accommodated Leiah's request.

Later that day, Evann, Leiah and I squeezed into an examination room. Leiah sat quietly in the corner, her head down. She had little energy, so I spoke for her. After I relayed her symptoms—fever, headache, and a new complaint, a sore throat—the doctor felt the nodes on Leiah's neck, checked her ears and throat, and took a throat swab. After ruling out mono, the doctor pronounced it most likely to be the flu. She prescribed Tylenol, five glasses of water each day, and told Leiah to expect to feel badly for about a week. When the doctor was about to leave, Leiah grunted and pointed at her face. I saw acne, which was usual for her, but it looked a little redder, almost like a rash. Unable to voice her concern, again I spoke for my daughter. "Doctor, Leiah is concerned about her face… her skin. What do you think?"

The doctor looked, pronounced it acne, and wrote a prescription. "This should help. If she isn't feeling better by Thursday, come back."

The next day, Wednesday, was my morning for Leaders Council at Community Bible Study. As a helper in the children's program, I would meet with the other leaders on Wednesday to get ready for class the following day. Since Leiah was able to pour her own cereal and juice that morning, I felt encouraged that she was improving, and was well enough to be on her own for a couple of hours. Assuring her I'd be back as soon as the meeting was over, I left. When I returned, Leiah told me she'd felt dizzy when she was in the bathroom and had fallen. Anxiously she begged me not to leave her alone again. Feeling guilty, I stayed close for the rest of the day. When I served her lunch—a poached egg and fruit salad to eat in front of the television— she seemed more lethargic and less communicative than the day before. For dinner she only managed a few forkfuls of French toast.

That night, her favourite show, *Party of Five*, was due to start at ten o'clock. Suggesting she sleep downstairs on the pullout couch so she could drift off when the show ended, I placed a glass of water on the end table beside the couch, and left to attend to chores. A little later, I returned to discover she had drifted off to sleep. Imagining how tired she must be not to stay awake for her favourite show, I turned off the television, tucked her in and headed upstairs, hoping one more good night's sleep was all she needed to turn around.

Part 2
the end of *before*

Thursday's Child

has far to go

At 7:20 the following morning, Thursday, I was awakened by Torey yelling. "Mom," she called, "Come quick—it's Leiah."

I sprinted downstairs and found Leiah on the family room floor. Her body was twisted around the legs of a toppled end table. My gaze moved to her face. Leiah's eyes looked vacant, and her lips were bitten. Scanning lower, I noticed her pants were wet. There was a gash on her left leg, with a shard of glass wedged in her calf. Frozen, I didn't know what to do. I called out, "David!" and knelt to do the only thing I could think to do: extract the piece of glass from her leg. As I did, her body started to quiver. I looked up and saw her mouth twitching. Her cheeks looked like they were being sucked inward. Her arms and legs began to flail.

What's happening? I wondered. Sensing David behind me I whispered, "What should we do?"

Calmly, he said, "Call 911."

I rushed to the kitchen phone and punched in the numbers. A woman's voice responded, "911. Fire, police or ambulance?"

"Ambulance. "

"What's happening?" the woman asked.

"She's on the floor...shaking...I think it's a...a...seizure... she's never had one...I've never seen one...she had the flu..."

The woman asked more questions. She sounded perplexed, as if something wasn't adding up. Finally she asked, "How old is the patient?"

"Fourteen," I cried. "She's only fourteen."

The woman's manner changed, growing crisper and sharper. She assured me help was on the way. I stood, holding the phone, not knowing what to do next. David offered practical advice, "Go upstairs...get dressed."

I did as I was told, returning downstairs minutes later to the sound of approaching sirens. Two firefighters were soon at Leiah's side, followed by paramedics. After assessing her condition, someone announced that they were taking her to Credit Valley Hospital.

I barely felt the cold of the early March morning as I followed the stretcher out the door and off to the hospital. Upon arrival she was whisked away. When I was allowed to see her, she was behind a curtained-off corner of the Emergency department. Her body was writhing on the bed and her face scrunched up, as if she was fighting something off. Garbled sounds spewed from her mouth, and her eyes remained unfocused. I longed to know what my daughter was thinking, feeling, and trying to say, but I couldn't understand anything. A man soon appeared at my side. He whispered, "I'm the head nurse. Let's step over here." When we were several feet away, he asked, "Is there anyone you need to notify?"

I looked at him blankly. *What was he asking? Notify? About what? Last night my daughter had the flu and this morning I wake up and everything has changed. I feel like I'm in the Twilight Zone. He can't possibly be saying…no…that's not possible.*

The nurse must have realized his question was too much for me to process. He spelled it out, "Your daughter is in serious condition. We don't know what is going to happen. If there are people who need to know, you need to call them now."

I gasped. Everything in me wanted to run from this place. Had it not been for the nurse's presence I might have, but he wouldn't let me. Quietly he ushered me into a tiny room and closed the door. On the table was a phone. I don't recall pushing buttons on the phone, but I must have called someone because people started showing up. My brother, Jim, Leiah's godfather, came first. He said not to worry, that he'd look after Torey and Evann, making sure they got fed, and taking them to and from school.

Meanwhile Leiah's condition confounded the doctors. A spinal tap and CT scan confirmed nothing. At one point the family doctor who had diagnosed the flu walked through the sliding doors, her eyes a mixture of shock and sympathy. Sometime after noon someone told me Leiah was going to the Hospital for Sick Children in downtown Toronto and we could meet her there.

Denial couldn't keep pace with the speed of unfolding events. Each new development tore another piece away from my mantle of false security.

After Leiah left by ambulance, David and I prepared to drive downtown. We stopped to buy a sandwich. I couldn't taste anything but I savoured the delay. Part of me knew there was no going back once we left the safety of our parked car. As we inched out into traffic I steeled myself for the chaos that lay ahead.

We found Leiah in a private room at the end of a corridor on the second floor of the Hospital for Sick Children's Critical Care Unit. Fearing she might be contagious, doctors had placed her in isolation. Everyone who entered her room had to wash their hands thoroughly and don a mask and robe. David and I sat by her bed, tensing each time her body writhed with a seizure. We began to time the space between each seizure. Unlike labour contractions, I hoped the spaces would grow farther apart. They didn't. Each time Leiah's body contorted I convinced myself it would be the last, but another seizure always followed. Sometimes the lapses grew longer, before sadistically shortening again. When the doctor arrived, he explained that each seizure was kindling a new one, the way embers in a fire jump from one burning twig to another, fanning a flame. With each new seizure I sank deeper into denial, convincing myself it would be the last, and that her brain still had billions of neurons that were working.

Waiting, wondering, worrying, and watching a parade of clinicians enter and exit was my lot that day—a long, dreadful day that sapped all of my energy. Sometime before midnight I pulled my Raggedy-Ann body out of the chair I'd been all but glued to, and shuffled to a waiting room where I lay down on a couch, pulled a blanket over my head, and slept.

Doctors continued to test for a vast array of viruses and bacteria, alongside a host of exotic diseases, such as cat scratch fever and mosquito-borne illnesses, but everything came back negative. I kept telling them, *No, she hadn't left the country.* I racked my memory for possible causes. *She'd fainted while getting her measles shot in middle school…could that be it?* "No," they said, "too long ago." I remembered something else. Leiah had been in orthodontic care for a few years. She'd worn a bionator, an apparatus that alters the position of the jaw, but the orthodontist said he couldn't install her braces until all of her baby teeth were out. Surprisingly, at age fourteen, a couple of upper baby teeth showed no sign of loosening, so the orthodontist suggested removing those teeth so he could apply braces sooner rather than later. Leiah didn't want to do it. She was adamant. Scared even. After some persuasion, she reluctantly agreed. When the dentist was pulling her teeth, she'd fainted in the dental chair. *It happened a couple of months ago. Could there be a latent infection?* Again they said, "No, too much time has elapsed."

The working diagnosis was viral encephalitis. Leiah was given an anti-viral medication, Acyclovir, in addition to antibiotics, just in case the cause was bacterial. *Encephalitis* means "acute inflammation of the brain" and can be caused by a virus or bacteria. The constant seizures complicated her condition. Dr. Shemie, her primary physician, advised that Leiah had sustained status epilepticus (SSE). Just as it sounds, with SSE the brain stays (status) in a persistent (sustained) state of seizure (epilepticus).

The doctors recommended putting Leiah into a drug-induced coma. They hoped it would give her brain time to heal, and bring the swelling down. It meant injecting her with a lot of drugs and hooking her up to a ventilator to help her breathe. What choice was there? We agreed.

That afternoon Dr. Shemie took us into a small room and told us more about sustained status epilepticus. He'd seen eight young people—girls and boys, more girls—with similar symptoms. Four had died, two became severely disabled, one was slightly disabled, and one had recovered. The odds were scary, but we believed Leiah would beat them. She would join the sole survivor to recover completely.

Leiah's father, Drew, arrived and sat vigil with David and me. March Break, the school holiday, was about to begin and David had been scheduled to fly to Alberta to visit his best friend. Leiah's condition nixed that plan. Halfway through the day we remembered something else. It was David's and my wedding anniversary, Friday March 13. Thumbing our noses at superstition, we'd thought it a lark to marry on that day. Today was another Friday the 13th. David and Drew grew hungry before I did, so the two of them left to share an anniversary dinner while I stayed by Leiah's side. It was weird but it didn't matter. Nothing was making sense anyway.

Perhaps in an effort to make a semblance of order in chaos, I decided to start a diary.

Part 3
diary

Diary

I am here alone for the first time since all this happened…We've been through the gamut of emotions since, and she through so many tests.

I've been touched by the outpouring of support and extent to which people are helping and offering assistance. She appears to have viral encephalitis, an inflammation of the brain. On this, Day 3, her fever came down, but she had another seizure this morning. Drew and his wife Ann are with her now.

***

This is day six of her seizures. I can't recall which day she went on the ventilator—perhaps Friday, perhaps Saturday. Today, as the chaplain put it, has not been a good day. Today, for the first time, it really hit home that she could die. The guilt? regret?

pain? I felt at not having appreciated the precious gift Leiah was and is hit me. Remembering how she asked me, "Mom, am I going to die?" last week, still makes me heave a heavy sigh, lamenting what might have been my last chance to hug her, *listen* to her and love her.

I am drained and weak. David has wanted to be my strength and it looks like he'll get his wish.

[Leiah was recently moved to a ward room with three other children after determining her disease was not infectious.]

The newborn baby boy across from her died today. His aunt said Sunday's Lenten reading was about the fig tree. Someone wanted to cut it down, but another person—the Lord, I expect—said, "No, wait…it will flower next year." I felt comfort when I heard those words. I tried to find the story in Evann's Bible, which I have with me, but I couldn't.

Ann Muckle [a friend from Trinity] came to visit today. She shared what one of our assistant priests had said about valleys. I guess I'm going through a valley. I don't know what is on the other side, or if I'm still going farther down. I think I was wrong when I told David's mom that it wasn't necessary to go to the bottom of the valley. This *is* the landscape. I can't just fly over it, although Jesus can carry me over the most horrendous parts. Instead I must walk through it. It will hurt. It will drain and exhaust me, but this is the landscape that God, in His wisdom, has put me in.

***

Thursday, March 19, 1998, 7:40 p.m.
I'm alone—well, by myself—at a table beside Starbucks, sipping a caramel macchiato and nibbling on a chocolate graham cookie that cost more than my dinner—a slice of veggie pizza and grapefruit juice.

I'm not sure how I'm dealing with all this. Maybe not very well, not in a healthy way. My friend Anne Armstrong called me a rock. I think I've blocked a lot of my life out of my mind, so that I almost forget I've got kids—in particular, one fourteen-year-old. If I forget, I won't miss her. But her smell follows me—the smell from the tubes in her nose and her mouth. That smell is always with me.

Today's weak moment was when I looked at her right hip bone jutting out. How fragile she looked.

I haven't prayed that much lately…I must do that.

Much of Leiah's treatment is a blur, as days merge into days. The physical manifestations of the seizures ceased today after they started pentothal, an anaesthetic which basically flatlines her brain activity. It also causes heart and blood pressure side effects. For those, she started dopamine yesterday and is now getting epinephrine, on top of the other meds: an anti-viral agent, acyclovar, antibiotics, erythromycin and phenobarbital. The plan now is to increase the phenobarbital level so they can wean her off pentothal, epinephrine and dopamine. The hope is that the change in treatment will allow her seizures to stop while they await additional test results and decide on the next step.

Yesterday's spinal tap and CT scan were normal. She had an MRI today and the initial reading appeared normal but a more detailed reading is being done tomorrow morning. The possibility of steroids is being considered, as is a brain biopsy, where a piece of brain tissue will be extracted and biopsied.

All we can do is go with the flow and not think about tomorrow except in hopeful terms.

It's just after eight p.m. I must be off now to say good night to Evann and Torey and perhaps to say a prayer.

***

Saturday, March 21, 1998, 2:50 a.m.

[The memory below was not recorded in my diary, but I remember it clearly.]

Friday night was tough. I was overcome with guilt that I had not been the mother Leiah deserved. All the years I'd spent working late when I should have been home with her to read a bedtime story…all the times I hadn't stepped away from what I was doing to listen to her talk… all the times I'd been hard on her. I'd damaged her self esteem and hadn't instilled in her a sense of how special she was. It was too much for me to bear. I became distraught. I didn't know how to live with myself.

David suggested I call [my friend] Anne Armstrong. It was late—after 9 p.m.—and she lived in Mississauga, about a forty-five-minute drive away. I didn't want to bother her, but I was desperate, so I picked up the phone and dialed. Anne had a headache, but when she heard how distraught I was, she asked her husband if he could drive her downtown, and he agreed. When Anne arrived we walked over to a Tim Horton's kiosk on the main level and chose a table.

I poured out my heart, my regrets, my fears and my inadequacies, and Anne listened. Then she told me something I will never forget. She said, "We all do the best we can with what we have at the time."

The words were a magic salve. I started to cry healing tears, as I recognized that my heart had never been that of an absentee mother. I loved my daughter. But I was damaged. I was confused. My priorities were messed up. When I gave birth to Leiah, I'd been badly hurt. I should have sought help then, but I didn't. I had thought only weak people got counselling. But now I saw that proud people who think they can manage on their own might be the ones who need help most.

As I reflected on the past fourteen years I realized I'd made plenty of mistakes, but I had done the best I could with what I had at the time. What I had was sadly lacking, yet what I had, I gave my daughter.

Anne's words let me see that I didn't have to stay stuck in this pit, drowning in regrets. Instead, I could acknowledge my inadequacies, many borne of circumstance, and move on. I had to in order to face the present.

I will be forever grateful for Anne's wise words, her compassion, and her presence that Friday night. Despite fatigue and headache, she (with the help of her faithful husband) made the trek downtown to sit with me into the wee hours of the morning. That is the mark of a true friend.

***

I am so glad David insisted I call Anne tonight. I got a lot off my chest and she has given me hope. She says she sees only good things happening from this. I believe Leiah will be healed—in God's time. I asked if He could hurry things up a bit but I do defer to His wishes.

Anne and I listened to a man who told us he is blessed to have a son whose name is Alex. I wondered why it was so important to him to share that his son was strong, until he dropped a bomb: Alex has Down syndrome. He glowed with pride when he showed us a photo of Alex. Indeed he is a beautiful child.

Anne says my gift is writing—not to be a teacher. I will ask God to guide me every day. I should try to get some sleep now.

***

Thursday, March 26, 1998, 11:20 p.m.
[This was the day Norm and Des shared the story of Abraham and Isaac and said it was a message from God for me.]

Tonight is the night of offering Leiah to God on the altar to show my fear of and faith in God. I prayed for a miracle, asking

43

God, who knows what is in our hearts, to grant us that desire and heal her, if it is His will. I believe, wish and hope it is His will to heal her.

Norm and Des may have told me the Abraham/Isaac story is mine, but I prefer the story of Jairus' daughter (as told in Matthew 9:18-25, Mark 5:21-43, and Luke 8:41-56). Here is Luke's version:

> *Then a man named Jairus, a synagogue leader, came and fell at Jesus' feet, pleading with him to come to his house because his only daughter, a girl of about twelve, was dying. As Jesus was on his way, the crowds almost crushed him. And a woman was there who had been subject to bleeding for twelve years, but no one could heal her. She came up behind him and touched the edge of his cloak, and immediately her bleeding stopped. "Who touched me?" Jesus asked. When they all denied it, Peter said, "Master, the people are crowding and pressing against you." But Jesus said, "Someone touched me; I know that power has gone out from me." Then the woman, seeing that she could not go unnoticed, came trembling and fell at his feet. In the presence of all the people, she told why she had touched him and how she had been instantly healed. Then he said to her, "Daughter, your faith has healed you. Go in peace." While Jesus was still speaking, someone came from the house of Jairus, the synagogue leader. "Your daughter is dead," he said. "Don't bother the teacher anymore." Hearing this, Jesus said to Jairus, "Don't be afraid; just believe, and she will be healed." When he arrived at the house of Jairus, he did not let anyone go in with him except Peter, John and James, and the child's father and mother. Meanwhile, all the people were wailing and mourning for her. "Stop wailing," Jesus said. "She is not dead but*

asleep." They laughed at him, knowing that she was dead. But he took her by the hand and said, "My child, get up!" Her spirit returned, and at once she stood up. Then Jesus told them to give her something to eat. Her parents were astonished, but he ordered them not to tell anyone what had happened. (Luke 8:41-56)

Perhaps because the main character was a girl, and who was only two years younger than Leiah, I identify more with this story than Abraham's and Isaac's. Also, Jairus' story is in the New Testament where Jesus saves the day. Why can't *that* story be ours…Leiah's and mine?

I am drained and tired. Drew keeps questioning, wondering if the doctors should have done an echocardiogram on her heart at the beginning. (Today the doctors told us they were concerned about her heart.) In retrospect, her heart may have been somewhat weak—she tired easily while playing soccer.

I want to go in and be with her to say, *Night-night, don't let the bed bugs bite and if they do, bite 'em back.*

Saturday, March 28, 1998, early a.m.
Leiah is still in critical condition. Last night, Thursday, Dr. Cox told us that Leiah's heart had been only functioning at six percent with no drugs, and twenty percent with drugs. Today she's at forty percent. That's a positive step. But her kidney function is down and her liver function is marginally improved. Dr. Cox prepared us for the worst. I cried. Drew sobbed. I prayed.

I'm very tired and confused now. I better wait until morning to continue.

***

Monday, March 30, 1998, early a.m.

On Sunday, when the doctors pulled a catheter out from within Leiah's heart, she experienced arrhythmia. Her heart beat three hundred times a minute, her blood pressure dropped to zero and she suffered cardiac arrest. Two to three minutes of manual massage re-started her heart. Curiously, although her phenobarbital levels are extremely high, still one eye responded slightly to light.

Hope amid horror.

***

Monday, March 30, 1998, 8:15 p.m.

I am alone for a little while. When I'm writing I don't feel alone. I want to write about this experience. I want to write about how nurses, especially critical care nurses, deserve respect and appropriate pay for all they do. When I can't bear to watch my daughter have another seizure, I can leave the room, take a walk, or even sometimes have a glass of wine. Her nurse must stay.

***

Tuesday, March 31, 1998, 11:05 a.m.

I just finished breakfast by the waterfall in the atrium where I read everything I'd written to date. I'll likely bring this book into Leiah's room so I can observe her and write things down there. Clinically her seizures aren't as jerky as they have been, but they are evident in her arms, shoulders and face. Her phenobarbital levels continue to drop so the seizures were to be expected. Her other vital signs are strong. They gave her some midazolam yesterday—from the valium family—which gives her short term relief from seizures via muscle relaxation.

The cause of the seizure kindling is still a mystery to the doctors. I suspected the initial cause was stress, until I just wrote that. I believe God has allowed this to happen so that lessons will be learned and growth will occur.

I just saw a new admission being wheeled into Critical Care, and my heart sank for the family that will be with him/her, wondering, worrying, crying and fearing. And yet we must count it all joy (James 1:2).

I pray for the Holy Spirit's peace to wrap Leiah in the cool embrace of His healing light— and that when it is time He will get in the middle of those kindling brain waves so they may rest and heal. Amen.

***

Thursday, April 2, 1998, 12:15 p.m.
[Reverend] Debbie Dennis, Gwen Eck and Anne Armstrong just left after praying through *Holy Communion* and *Ministry of Healing to the Sick* on Leiah. Debbie says she's seen people look a lot sicker than Leiah who still survived. The neurologist was walking by when I left the room, and basically said that chances for a good outcome were gone. That's when fear took root in me. I wondered if God was punishing me for a past sin. I asked Debbie if this could be my penance. Debbie said she could not serve a God who would do that. I sobbed uncontrollably in Debbie's presence while I finally admitted my deepest fear— that I might lose Leiah. Debbie told me she would *never* forget that.

***

Sunday, April 5, 1998, almost midnight
Today Leiah looked quite pale. She was "stooling" and "peeing" a lot and her hemoglobin went down to 8.3, I believe, so they transfused her with red blood cells. I felt depressed today, although a picture of Leticia's mother [someone I met in

hospital] just came to mind saying, "Keep the high faith. She'll be okay." Certainly so many people's *feelings* were that she'd be okay. Today I wondered if that meant okay in life, or okay in heaven. I know she'll be okay in heaven, but I'd prefer she not be going there now.

Her seizures are quite violent. They include her stomach and both hands turn claw-like. I just found out the little girl across from Leiah died, that she was actually brain-dead since this morning but they had kept her alive on a respirator. No wonder the whole family was there and that the mom would periodically moan, "My baby…"

***

Wednesday, April 8, 1998, 2 a.m.

[Apart from one brief trip home, I lived at the hospital. David stayed when he could, as he was trying to manage things on the home front, along with the help of friends and family. Our younger daughters Torey and Evann had not yet visited Leiah, although they did later on. In some ways I regret letting them see her, as the sight of their unmoving sister hooked up to tubes may have been traumatic. Drew was there most days. His wife, Ann, was frequently there. Initially we all slept on couches in various waiting rooms. During the first week, we noticed people coming and going from a room along the back wall of the Critical Care Unit waiting room. We learned that a family had been staying in that room ever since their son had undergone an emergency heart transplant. Several days later, we noticed family members moving their belongings out of the room. That afternoon we were offered the space. Although pleased with the space and privacy the room afforded, there was a frightening undercurrent: staying in that room meant our child's life was in greater danger than we cared to admit. The room accommodated two pull-out couches, side by side, separated by a

pillar. I shared the room with Drew, and David would sleep over on weekends and at other times. Leiah's illness had made for strange bedfellows.

The dire circumstances had opened up lines of communication which had been all but closed for years. I saw friends and family from my first marriage, current in-laws, former-in-laws, new friends and old. I got to know my ex-husband's wife and family, and came to appreciate them, and their caring for my daughter. It was touching to listen to Ann read storybooks to Leiah, and I felt like Ann's sister and brother-in-law were my own in-laws. It was a weird, yet ironically wonder-filled time, when the pain we shared turned a key that gently reopened an old door, one that had slammed shut years earlier when my first marriage ended. Leiah's extended illness provided time and space to smooth out frazzled ends of unfinished conversations and pour salve on open wounds. There was no time for small talk, only real, heart-to-heart conversation. It was like being on holy ground.

Scores of people visited, some of whom I barely knew. One person had contracted encephalitis or possibly meningitis as a teen. In a coma for weeks, she wasn't expected to survive. As she told me her story, I noticed she had to stop several times while she was talking. I figured it was hard for her to relive it. She said she had heard everything and felt every touch while she was in the coma. She thoroughly disliked one nurse, who handled her roughly and spoke unkindly, and much preferred caregivers who spoke and touched her gently. This story gave me hope that Leiah too would emerge from her coma and that she was aware of all the care around her.]

Today was a difficult day. Leiah had an MRI at 8 a.m. and when I pushed Dr. Foong for results after his 3 p.m. meeting, he told me there was "diffuse damage to the brain" (meaning it was all over, not isolated to just one side). Sometimes I think that if it was only in one part of her brain, she'd be okay. He said the evoked potential test which they had also done was only a crude tool to see whether the neurons were talking to each other. The test couldn't tell whether or not what the neurons were saying to each other was gibberish.

Dr. Bohn spoke to David, Ann and me in the classroom around five p.m. He explained that yes, the damage was extensive, but that it didn't look the same as the MRI of a girl who had been in a few months before. In Leiah's case there wasn't a covering over the cells, like the one a virus would leave, yet it didn't seem to look like vasculitis (an inflammation of blood vessels). He suggested a brain biopsy was basically the last chance—in his opinion—to diagnose the cause. However, he said, there was a great likelihood that no diagnosis would be made and that even if one was arrived at, no treatment may exist for it. There's a miniscule—less than miniscule—possibility that both a diagnosis and treatment could be suggested. Most likely, he said, they could make a prognosis if a diagnosis was made.

Leiah didn't tolerate her liquid formula food today: it went right through her. Her seizures have more space between them, yet five minutes seems about the maximum lapse. Her temperature was lower this morning but it was high tonight—39.9 degrees under the armpit.

I gave twenty dollars to a guy on the street named Valentine tonight. He showed me his feet and said, "See my feet aren't strong enough to work."

[Reverend] Debbie Dennis says people who told me to *keep the faith* that Leiah will be all right may have been giving me the hope I needed to sustain me through *that* day. Debbie is still praying for a miracle but believes I should be listening to everything the doctors say.

My hope seems to be a thin strand now—or a *shard,* as Anna says. I can only pray for guidance.

***

Thursday, April 9, 1998, 12:30 a.m.

Another difficult day with a lot of tough things to consider. I had a long talk with Dr. Durwood. Miracles, he says, don't happen that often. For every miracle that you read about in the paper, there are many more situations that don't turn out that way.

Today I accepted—on some levels—that Leiah may not make it. And yet I think of what [my friend] Lynn said—*not to give up on her*. She said, "This is real prove-you're-a-great-mother stuff."

And just how do I do that? I know any decisions I make will have to be for her best interest—things *she* would want. I just thought of how awful she'd feel if she heard and understood my talking about organ donation—that she might think I couldn't wait for her to go. How awful that would be. Lord, I pray that if she did hear, that You would wipe it from her memory.

Lynn performed therapeutic touch on Leiah and told me she didn't feel fear from Leiah; she felt strength.

The nurses asked for photos of Leiah, so they could see who she was before her illness. David brought some photos of her skiing and other pictures with friends and family. We posted them by her bed. They were a stark contrast to the gaunt girl who lay immobile on the bed.

When I asked what I should and shouldn't say to Leiah, the social worker said to follow my heart and say what I feel I should to her.

Today I recalled the story Leiah wrote a few months ago about a girl and her mom who seemed very close to each other until the mother was killed in a car accident. I remembered the day she read the story to me. She had walked into my bedroom, and stood beside me as she read. When she finished the story, I had asked why she had called it *My Guardian Angel.* She told me that the girl saw an angel on her bed which helped pull her through her sadness at losing her mom. Then, she said, the girl met 'a nice man'. I asked who the nice man was. *Was it the girl's birth father? Did she end up living with him?* Leiah had had a faraway look as she considered my question. "No," she said. "Not him. Someone else. But the girl is okay…she's fine." This is her story:

My Guardian Angel

"Vanessa, come on, we're going to be late for the Christmas party," my mother Dianne called.

"I'll be there in a minute, I'm just finishing up my makeup. Mrs. Elson said her nephew Adam is going to be there and he's thirteen as well."

"All right, just hurry, please."

My mom and I were very close. She's been like my best friend since I was born. My dad left us when I was only two years old. I don't remember anything about him, all I know is that my mom has always been there for me!

I quickly ran down the stairs. I was so excited about this party. I thought it would be the best night I ever had, especially since I was going to see Adam and he's like drop dead gorgeous.

"Alright, let's hit the road," I said excitedly.

"Finally," my mom said grinning.

I threw on my jacket, then we climbed into the car then drove off. It was about a twenty minute drive to the Elsons' house. We had been driving for about five minutes when I said, "Mom, do you think Adam will notice me tonight?"

"Of course he will, you look beautiful."

"Thanks, so do you," I replied back.

My mom smiled at me and then turned on some Christmas music and started to sing along to them.

"Are we there yet?" I asked about ten minutes later.

"Just a bit longer."

We were approaching a red light then. It turned green so my mom continued to go through as we sang Deck the Halls, when I suddenly blurted out, "Mom! A car!!!"

She looked over but it was too late. Smack right into the driver's side.

"Nooooo!" I screamed, then I got knocked out.

I woke up to daylight in a hospital bed. I looked around the bare room. There was no sign of my mom. "Where is she?" I whispered to myself as a single tear ran down my cheek. I climbed out of bed and looked down to find a cast on my leg and I was in a great deal of pain. Although I didn't care. I just had to find my mom. I limped out into the hallway. I saw sick people coming up and down hallways, nurses, doctors, but where was my mom?

"Vanessa." Someone called to me. I turned around and noticed a tall woman in a white outfit coming toward me. I assumed she was a nurse. As she approached me she asked, "What are you doing out of bed? You need your rest!" She helped me walk back into my room, and climb into bed. I looked at her with a teary face and asked, "Where's my mom?"

The nurse looked at me with a sad face.

"No!" I cried.

"I'm sorry, Vanessa."

"No, she's fine. Tell me where she is," I cried louder.

"I'm very sorry," the nurse continued. "She didn't make it."

"No, she's fine, she is not dead!" I cried even louder then burst into tears. The nurse bent over and gave me a hug.

"I'm sorry." She cried as well. "I'm really sorry!" Then the nurse stood up. "I'll give you some time alone, just call if you need me. My name is Nancy."

She left the room and closed the door behind her. "I can't believe this," I said. "Two days before Christmas Eve. This is the worst Christmas ever!" Then I burst into tears and then fell asleep, hoping I would wake up and it was all a dream.

***

Good Friday, April 10, 1998, just before 1 a.m.

Last night's dream was horrible. I actually can't remember the details right now, but— wait, now I do—the resuscitator was pulled off Leiah. Rather than passing peacefully away, as Dr. Durwood said was possible, she gasped and writhed until she stopped breathing. Her heart stopped but the seizures continued. I touched her chest and felt no heartbeat yet watched her body continue to seize. I thought, *how unfair—I'd made the decision to withhold artificial life support and lose my living, breathing daughter, and still those seizures kept control of her body.*

The seizures are like demons, giving her body no peace and robbing her mind of thoughts, communication and understanding. It's just like the day last year, when she writhed in pain on the floor of the living room, moaning and groaning, "I never felt special—never!" The words cut through me then and haunt me now. Perhaps all that pain inside her welled up until it made her sick? Maybe it crept secretly, like one of those viruses that can't be detected, waiting until the moment was ripe to attack her mind? A flu virus likely weakened her and that pain worked from the inside out, undetected in the first tests, but causing seizure upon seizure upon seizure, damaging the cells that govern memory and coordination.

She had her brain biopsy today. The surgeon hadn't wanted to do it. He felt there was no point. He said it was an operation that wouldn't make any difference in her prognosis. My cousin, Elizabeth, a nurse, once told me that surgeons were all the same. Their motto was, "If I can cut it, I can fix it." I guess he figured there was no point in cutting if he couldn't fix it. When I found out he didn't want to operate, I went to meet him. There he was, safely behind a desk, his face impassive, until a sunray beamed through the window behind him, highlighting his face. His eyes, hidden behind reading glasses, reminded me of my father's—light blue and kind. I told him the biopsy was our last chance to find out why this had happened. If there was any clue a biopsy could shed on the cause of Leiah's illness, I needed to know it. I begged him to do the procedure. It wasn't until tears of resignation welled in my eyes that he pulled his glasses off, looked at me, and said, "Okay, I'll do it."

Now we must wait.

A miracle happened later today. My unbelieving husband David cried at Movenpick [restaurant] and said he wanted to go to Trinity [church]. Leiah allowed this miracle to transpire. Now, will God heal her brain—or at least partly heal it?

Tuesday, April 14, 1998, approximately 1:30 a.m.

[My handwriting for this notation is hard to decipher, yet it appears I wrote, "I prayed a lot tonight—that we'd be painting a blue room vs. that other house." *I'm not certain what I meant by "that other house", but it probably refers to Jesus saying* "In my Father's house there are many mansions: if it were not so, I would have told you. I go to prepare a place for you" *(John 14:2, KJV). Modern versions substitute "rooms" for "mansions." I suspect the "blue room" was Leiah's room at home, which was still builder's beige. I probably meant that as soon as she got out of hospital, we would go home and paint her room whatever colour her heart fancied.]*

As long as there is life there is hope.

Charlene [my sister] says that [her brother-in-law] Bill's dad had kept saying that line to his daughter Peg, while she was sitting beside her husband's bedside for six weeks being told by doctors that he wouldn't make it. He did. Tricia, Leiah's nurse today, spoke those same words.

I have more hope today, although I have had moments of sadness. In Cultures [restaurant] tears came to my eyes. At Tim Horton's I saw Mrs M [whose son had a heart transplant]. She was all dressed up like she'd returned to work. I almost went over to her to say that if Leiah didn't make it, I was considering donating her heart. But I didn't go. Shyness? Or was I worried about invading her personal space?

Leiah seems more wakeful today. Her eyes open by themselves. But her pupils are large and I don't see any recognition there. The downside is that her seizures seem more frequent, with less space between them. Sometimes she breathes partly on her own and the ventilator is just assisting her. Today I saw the beginnings of a cough reflex.

David doesn't know what to make of it. He doesn't want to change his realism over to hope unless the doctors give him good reason. Not many doctors around today.

Tuesday, April 14, 1998, noon

I'm here at Starbucks with my skinny latte and blueberry scone. Leiah's seizures are continuing. The only change in plan is to put a new line in her arm because the scapula line is apparently a "portal for infection." Dr. Foong says he's trying to get all the information together for a meeting this afternoon. The information from neuropathology might actually be back today.

I was just thinking. Leiah has kept everybody waiting all her life. Why should things change now? Early on in the pregnancy I almost miscarried but I rested and had to wait until the risk passed. She also survived surgery I had at five months gestation [to stitch up an "incompetent cervix"]. And she didn't tumble out, as expected, when the stitches came out a week before her due date. I had to go home and wait until she was ready.

My mom has always said, "Good things come to those who wait." I had to wait until September 30, 1983 at 2:24 p.m. to see those big blue eyes look back at me.

***

I remember the delivery room at St. Michael's Hospital. It was cold. While I was being prepared for surgery a nurse asked if I'd picked out a name. Grateful for an opportunity to share, I replied, "Russell James Andrew for a boy, and Leiah Christine Anne for a girl." Russell was the name of a writer uncle on my father's side, James was my brother's name, and Andrew was Drew's given name. As for the female choice, Drew's paternal grandmother was named Leah. I'd never met her but I'd read some of her letters and sensed they were penned by a warm, loving woman. I modified the spelling of her name for two reasons: when I had gone to see *Star Wars Return of the Jedi* while pregnant, the character Princess Leia intrigued me. She had moxy. I also liked the way her name looked and sounded, with three vowels in a row. Secondly, the name *Leah* means "weak-eyed tired cow." How could I tell my daughter we had named her for a near-sighted weary bovine? *Leiah* was the perfect solution: a blend of both names.

Christine, her middle name, was a middle name of my maternal grandmother, and first name of my sister Nichole. Anne was a family name passed down from my maternal great grandmother to my mother to me, as a middle name.

When Dr. Louis Burgener pulled the baby out and pronounced, "It's a girl," tears welled in my eyes. I hadn't realized how much I'd hoped for a girl. Nurses transferred her to a table a few metres away where she stared back at me with knowing eyes.

Her face resembled my own baby pictures—round, full cheeks, pointy chin and blue eyes, but she had light brown hair whereas I'd been bald. I don't know why, but for some reason this thought came to me, *My life is starting again in her*. Meanwhile Drew lamented that he couldn't see anything of himself in his daughter's face. "She has your nose, your ears, your chin…"

As the doctor stitched up my belly, I heard my baby's stats: eight pounds, five and a half ounces and twenty-two inches long, Her Apgar scores were nine at one minute and a perfect ten four minutes later. Her score elicited my first burst of mother's pride. When my swaddled daughter was presented to me, I started to cry. My tears were joyful, but they also signalled a cathartic release of tension. The tears jarred something and my nose started to bleed. (My blood pressure was sky high prior to her birth, and I suffered severe nosebleeds as a result.) A nurse took my daughter and an orderly wheeled me to another corner of the hospital where an ear, nose and throat specialist cauterized my nose, stuffed it with gauze, and bandaged it. My daughter might have scored a ten but my new mom photos ranked a minus three.

***

And now we are waiting again. I pray that the Lord will give me the questions to ask the doctors, and that Leiah gets her heart's deepest desire, and that it may be God's will. Actually, is the heart's deepest desire God's will? Is the soul's desire God's will?

It's in your hands, Lord.

***

Wednesday, April 15, 1998, 2:15 a.m.
I was in Leiah's room for a long time. I started to see life in her left eye—and tears. The nurse saw a hair in her eye. An explanation for the tears. To her, at least. I see tears and grimaces. Leiah must be exhausted.

Tracey, the nurse, and the other nurse say the midazolam and morphine should keep Leiah less aware of her surroundings. She says most kids who re-visit the ICU don't remember the nurses and what it's like there. (Not initially maybe, but later?)

I'm tired and irrational tonight, but emotional too. It's been almost five weeks of seizures. It makes me think of my last five weeks of being pregnant with Leiah, and the day everything changed...

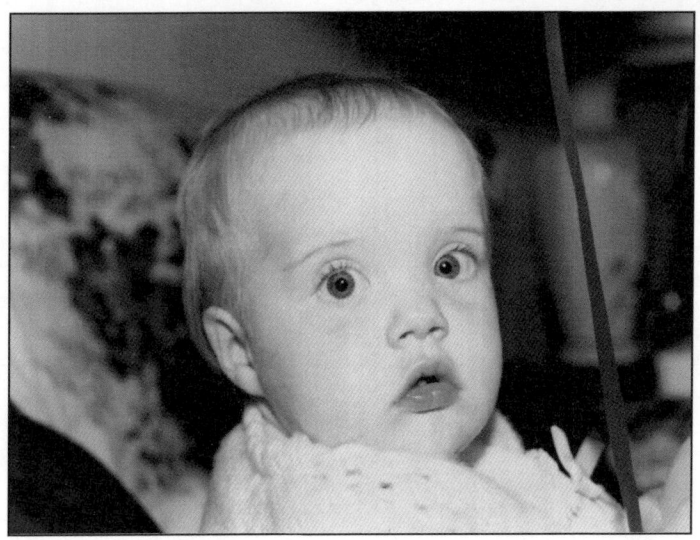

Leiah in full Tweety Bird visage, age 1

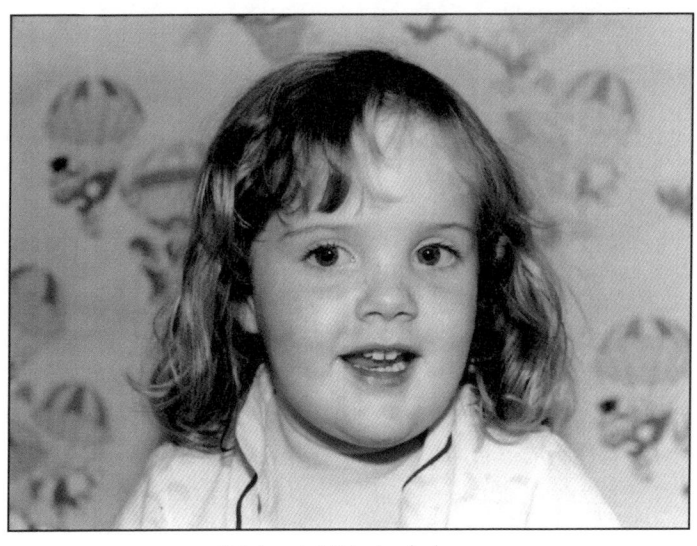

Leiah at 1-1/2 in her bedroom

Enjoying a swim at age 2

On a rocky reservoir beach in Calgary, Alberta, at age 5-1/2

*Leiah's blue coat setting off her deep blue eyes,
atop Sulphur Mountain, Banff, Alberta, almost 6*

Cousin Brett, 9, beside Leiah, 10, with Evann, 1, on her hip

My three daughters on the stairs:
Torey, 5, Evann, 2 and Leiah, 11, holding Hammy

Ready for Grade 7, almost 12

A proud mom standing beside her beautiful daughter,
almost 14, on Grade 8 Graduation day

The sketch Leiah drew of Evann, 5, Torey, 8 and herself,
14 with an admonition "Do not throw out"

Watercolour Leiah painted in 1998 of angelic being with long brown hair in a
purple dress lying atop a cloud

All smiles – a newly minted teen

Leiah in her usual pose, happily chatting to a friend on the phone

Leiah in her soccer uniform as a pre-teen.

Part 4

detouring into the past

Late
august, 1983

At almost eight months pregnant I'd hurried home from work to catch the last ten minutes of *The Young & the Restless,* a soap opera I'd kept tabs on since I was in my teens. Lounging on the brown corduroy couch in the basement, I was admonishing a character for yet another stupid choice when I heard Drew's steps on the basement stairs. Soon he was in front of me, looking like he had something to say. I nodded but kept my concentration on Nikki Newman, the onscreen character.

He cleared his throat and spoke, "I have something to tell you."

I looked up. His face looked different, closed and hard. Obviously something was on his mind. "Okay," I began, "what is it?"

He paused a moment, then blurted out his news. "I'm seeing someone else."

What?! Did he just say there's someone else? I looked down and touched my belly. *But I'm pregnant…we're married. We're supposed to be a family…*

"I'm sorry. I didn't mean for it to happen. It just did," he continued, his face devoid of warmth.

I started to panic. *What did this mean? Was our marriage over? Was I to bring up this baby alone? How could I? What would I do? Why had this happened? No!* As *The Young & the Restless* theme played, I realized I was now living in my own soap opera. It was not a role I knew and I didn't play it well.

***

Having a child had not been on the table for Drew and me, until *maybe* sometime in the future. Married for two-and-a-half years, I was twenty-six and Drew was four years my senior. We lived in a small house in Unionville, Ontario, northeast of Toronto.

To say we weren't close is a bit like saying Antarctica and Greenland are *a little* far apart on the globe. Our communication was the pits. We'd become experts at denial and wilful blindness, and had perfected the art of sweeping events and feelings under the rug.

Normally Drew and I went our separate ways after dinner, but one night in January could only be described as an anomaly. Spanish coffee was my domain, but only if we had company. That night Drew shocked me by suggesting and preparing Spanish coffee for the two of us. The haze that enveloped us was not, however, alcoholic. It was otherworldly. We drank, we talked, we laughed. We actually seemed to like—even love— each other. It was like being in a bubble where only truth and loving words were possible. Something was in the air. I wanted a baby—deeply. I knew he did not, at least not yet. I was honest with him and told him there was a chance of conceiving. And he said he didn't care—perhaps out of passion alone, perhaps out of more than that. (John 1:12-13 gives me a possible explanation for God's plan for this evening.)

Our marriage returned to its regularly scheduled programming the next day—distant, depressed and defensive. When, six weeks later a blood test confirmed I was pregnant, I was understandably nervous about how Drew would react. I considered a delay tactic inspired by the *I Love Lucy* show— keeping the pregnancy a secret and surprising him with a baby eight months later. Instead I told him with a book. After he read the title, *Becoming a Father*, he ran out of the house. It was not the idyllic moment I'd dreamed of. Eventually he came around…or at least seemed to.

***

The last five weeks of my pregnancy were among the hardest of my life. The not knowing, the thinking about how I could "win him back," plagued me. I had terrible dreams that our baby was born much too skinny, half-deaf and half-blind, with breathing problems, and that he died.

I worried that my sleeplessness and anxiety would hurt the baby and I did everything I could to help myself sleep and find peace of mind. I kept a diary during that time and wrote, "God must figure in all this, and have a reason for it all happening. It just escapes me for the moment. However, I believe He wants us to mature from the experience and become more full human beings, especially since He is entrusting us with the gift of a child."

Stress consumed me so much so that I had to start my maternity leave early. I slept less, worried more, ate little, and as a result, my blood pressure rose sky high. My nose had felt dry throughout my pregnancy and I'd suffered occasional nosebleeds, but they started to become much worse. Sometimes I'd lean over a sink until red covered the bottom, then collapse from blood loss. I had never felt so weak… so barely alive. When I wasn't angst-filled about Drew leaving, I was guilt-ridden that my anxiety/not eating/not sleeping might be harming the baby.

My doctor assured me that babies are effective parasites, taking what they need.

Everyone thought stress would bring labour on, but it didn't. A week before my due date, my doctor ordered me to hospital where he removed the sutures he'd put in at five months gestation. Drew and I waited, expecting the baby to tumble out. It didn't.

The following week, my nosebleeds grew worse, depleting any remaining physical reserves. The doctor sent me to the hospital where he ordered an ultrasound, the first since early in the pregnancy. The scan uncovered the reason the baby hadn't tumbled out the week before. The baby was in breech position—bottom first.

This news meant a change in plans: the doctor recommended a Caesarian section.

It was another disappointment. First my marriage and then my dreams for giving birth naturally. But I didn't really have a choice. A C-section was scheduled for the following afternoon, Friday, September 30. The doctor asked if I wanted Drew in the room. My instinct was to say "no." Just having him nearby was stressful. But it was his firstborn child so I buried my angst and gave my consent.

Although we witnessed her birth together, it was not enough to bind us. We'd grown too far apart and all the recent pain and confusion muddled things more.

Nine days later Drew picked both of us up from hospital, dutifully deposited us at the house, and left. Nine days later I left that house with my baby. But before I left, something remarkable happened.

***

I was in Leiah's room, standing in front of her change table when something compelled me to fall to my knees. Closing my eyes, a picture of a lone goat on a dark, misty mountaintop appeared in my mind's eye. I sensed a kinship with the animal. Like it, I felt lost, alone and exhausted from a solitary trek along rocky terrain. I wanted to go home, but didn't know how to get there. Digging deep into my soul, I pressed upon something that released a torrent of emotion.

I don't…I can't do this anymore. I feel so far away… from what, I don't know. I only know I feel lost. I need…something…

My heart started to hurt. I was connecting to something deep down inside me—something I didn't even know was there. As I continued to pour out my feelings, thoughts started to occur. I recalled things I'd done, words I'd said, choices I made. At the time I'd thought they were simply choices—neither good nor bad—just things everybody was doing. At that moment I saw many of those choices for what they were: *sin*.

Ironically, on some level, I don't think I believed *sin* was real. Sometimes I'd laughingly say so-and-so was "living in sin," but I didn't actually believe they were doing something wrong. After all, (almost) everybody was doing it. I couldn't imagine that a divine being considered our choices to be abhorrent. Such a mocking attitude had caused me to blur lines between right and wrong. I realized that when I had made a really bad choice, I would rationalize that others had chosen worse than I. I'd also misunderstood *guilt*, believing it to be the product of an overactive conscience, not something that truly exists. On my knees, I recalled choices I had made and felt guilt. It was not a pleasant sensation. The pain was horrid. I could not bear it. I had to get it off of me.

I confessed things I'd done which I now realized were wrong. I said how sorry I was for the hurt my actions had caused others, myself, and, ultimately, God. Then something marvellous happened. It was an experience akin to Tinkerbell flying through Peter Pan's window. I sensed a light streaming through Leiah's bedroom window and resting upon me. When it did, all the angst, worries and hopelessness that had plagued me every moment of the day for the last two months simply fell away, leaving in their place the most perfect feeling of peace I had ever felt. With little basis for comparison, I thought back to how it felt to try marijuana as an anxious teen. It had been a light, relaxing feeling that took me away from my worries, but that feeling was nothing like what I was experiencing now. *This* peace felt pure and honest, full of love and life. The other was counterfeit.

For the first time in months, perhaps years, angst and worry didn't occupy my every thought. Words came to mind— *the hour I first believed*—then a song title—*Amazing Grace*. I remembered I owned a Joan Baez album with that song on it.

I floated downstairs, put the record on the turntable, and listened to Baez sing *Amazing Grace* again and again. Soaking up the words, I was awestruck by how they described exactly what had just happened to me. I was a wretch…I was blind…I was lost…my heart didn't fear God. But I sought Him with all my heart, without even realizing what I was doing—and He let Himself be found. The peace resting upon me was one that *passed understanding*. It was a peace that *relieved all my fears*.

I now had empirical proof: God was indeed real. Not only was He real, He was the source of true peace.

Listening to *Amazing Grace* over and over allowed me to revel in the grace that brought me to that point in time. I recognized several snares and dangers I had passed through and was grateful. The pure, glorious feeling of peace lasted an hour, before starting to dissipate. The memory of that hour remains a gift I shall always cherish. May the words from *Amazing Grace* never ring hollow to me and to all who experience such grace.

***

I was not free of snares for long. The joy of a new baby was dampened by anxiety and depression which once again took root and held my mind captive. While I had been in hospital, in a bright room with windows, meals, nurses, and joyful new parents, I ate well, slept soundly and took excellent care of my baby. Back in the house where my world had crumbled, I sensed mostly darkness. Without another adult to share the load and help me to control my meandering thoughts, I sank deeper into depression and once again stopped eating and sleeping. Yet I didn't share the extent of my true state with anyone, for fear someone would take my baby away.

Leiah was about three weeks old and a public health nurse was supposed to visit us. I was afraid she would come, assess me as unfit to care for my baby, and take Leiah away. Early that morning I called my mother, sobbing and spilling out my fears. Fortunately my mother took charge, admonishing me to *hold on*. Mom told me she would cancel the appointment with the Public Health Nurse, and would make arrangements to pick Leiah and me up so that we could stay with her.

Peace and support were mine at last. I could finally exhale.

***

Leiah and I stayed at my mom and stepdad's house for the rest of my maternity leave. It was healthier for both of us. Stick-thin and emotionally fragile, I needed help looking after myself and my daughter. I got it. It was a full house. Only my sister, Charlene, had moved out (I also have a sister, Cindy, from my father's second marriage). My parents and other siblings, Jim, Nichole and Grant, all loved having Leiah around, except when her crying woke them up. Everyone pitched in with feeding, diaper changing, and winding up her baby swing to calm her. Each formed a special bond with her.

***

Drew had moved back into our house while Leiah and I were at Mom's. One day I suggested to him that Leiah and I would drive over for a visit. At the time I owned a car with a few idiosyncrasies, one of which was that it would stall without warning, especially in the rain.

It was raining lightly. We traversed Highway 401 East without incident, but a minute after merging on to Hwy. 404 northbound, my car stalled in the centre lane. Frantic, I put on my four-way flashers and prayed that drivers would see us in time to change lanes. I cringed as I caught many cars swerving at the last second. I tried to start the car, but it would not respond. I was helpless.

When I was brave enough to look into my rearview mirror again I glimpsed a giant tow truck behind me. A man's face was soon at my window. I rolled it down.

"I saw your car…then I saw the baby, so I had to stop," he said.

"Thank God. Thank you so much. Can you tow me?"

"I tow big trucks, but I radioed for a smaller truck. It's on the way."

As my saviour left to stand rear guard I turned to check on Leiah. She was a picture of contentment, blowing bubbles through her lips, oblivious to the drama. Even before I read the verse that said, "*See that you do not despise one of these little ones. For I tell you that their angels in heaven always see the face of My Father in heaven*" (Matthew 18:10), I had heard.that children had their own guardian angels. Leiah's angel was on duty that morning; I got saved by proxy.

When my maternity leave ended, Leiah and I moved back into the house in Unionville. We lived on our own for about a year before Drew returned unannounced. He had nowhere to go, and since the house was half his, I didn't have a right to refuse. We lived separately—he had the basement, and Leiah and I were upstairs—but whenever we met on the main floor, it was stressful. Other than one session with a social worker, the two of us had never talked out our issues. So much was left unsaid. We developed many hard feelings—ones that became more deeply buried as the years passed—until fourteen years later we had to face one another again.

Part 5
back to the future

Diary
april, 1998

Wednesday, April 15, 1998, 2:15 a.m.
But why, why should Leiah have to suffer?

She's such a perfect sacrifice.

Will God take her?

What miracle will there be?

I'm tired. That's all—except I got mad at Drew today. When we were sitting in the parent room, talking about potential outcomes, I asked about him paying the premium for any long term health care for Leiah if she survived with a disability. He said he couldn't, as he wouldn't have a job. His reaction was a trigger that threw me back fourteen years to when he fled responsibility. I started to fume. I couldn't sit in his presence a moment longer. I had to get out. I strode out the door and out on to the street, circling the block, over and over, until my anger dissipated.

Today, Leiah's friend, Sharon, came to see her. Sharon sat by Leiah's bed for three hours, telling her about all the news in her life, and what was going on in the lives of their mutual friends. Sharon described the weather that day and set the scene outside her window, so that Leiah might imagine it.

[Years later Sharon told me she stayed all those hours because she couldn't bear to leave Leiah's side a moment earlier. After Sharon had said everything she came to say, and had sat long enough by her dear friend's side, only then was she able to get up and leave.]

***

Monday, April 20, 1998

On Friday April 17, Ann, David, Rose [Leiah's nurse], Tricia [social worker] and I met with Dr. Shemie. He told us Leiah would either die, or live in a vegetative state. He asked us, "Would she want that?" After he spoke, I felt like I was in freefall in a deep, dark pit, until finally I grabbed on to something. I didn't want to open my eyes to acknowledge what held me, because the very thing that held me was what I was being asked to let go of. I knew the answer to his question, yet I could not voice it. So I did what I could. I mouthed the word and shook my head *no*, to signify she would not want to live that way.

After the meeting, David and I left the hospital. He thought it would be a good idea to get away so he booked a room at a nearby hotel. Yet there was no escape. In some ways I felt worse outside of the hospital, because I was disconnected from Leiah. I felt so empty and sad, knowing that on Sunday or Monday we would be making arrangements to take Leiah off the respirator. But Drew wasn't ready. Although Drew and I spoke one night—was it last Tuesday?— about funerals, burials, and his concern about an autopsy, Drew refused to accept it might come to pass. The last time we met with Michael, the hospital chaplain, Michael told Drew, David and me to consider

Leiah's body as a potential vessel for discovering the cause of this disease and possibly helping others. An autopsy, he said, was simply another "operation" and her body would be treated with the same respect.

Today the decision was made to unhook her respirator on Thursday afternoon.

***

Tuesday, April 21, 1998, 9:20 a.m.

Alone in the parents' room of the back of the Critical Care Unit waiting area. I've decided to write my "morning papers." In my dreams I gave birth to a son, who seemed healthy but later developed problems, life-threatening ones. At the same time Leiah was in my dream. She came in for simple routine surgery on her abdomen, I think, but it kept progressing and progressing, to the point where she was barely alive? Or maybe she was gone. I remember being so heartbroken about losing my first and last children at the same time, but then coming back to the hospital and finding out, no, they were still alive.

Should I have hope that this will change?

Drew just called. He wants to meet with someone from the bioethics committee. I thought he was ready to have a meeting with Dr. Shemie where we could discuss all the questions he had: *Is it really necessary to do an autopsy? How much information will it yield? More than the brain biopsy? What about DNA testing?* His theory is that together Drew and I may have made her into a walking time bomb. *Fact or fiction?*

But unless the bioethics meeting can be held soon, followed by the doctor's meeting about what precisely will be done at the time of withdrawal of life support, this may mean we must wait another day. [We later met with someone from bioethics but I didn't learn anything new.]

I pray that God will direct all our hearts, words, minds—our entire beings—towards His perfect will in all things, but especially in regard to Leiah.

***

Wednesday, April 22, 1998, 10:40 a.m.

I felt weak and shaky before I ate, and read "Someone Cares," a booklet of inspirational paragraphs and quotes from the Bible. It's hard to reconcile hope with medical likelihood.

Regarding healing, it says sometimes God heals you through medicine, or sometimes directly in answer to a special prayer. No matter what, God is the Great Physician. He may choose to make others well by taking Leiah, or He may choose to heal her directly and in so doing, affect people by that miracle.

My mission—should I choose to accept it—would seem to be to choose the latter (that He will heal her directly). I shall keep *that* hope and only to change it to the former (that He will *take* Leiah), *if* that is required.

God knows what is best. Thank you, Lord.

***

Thursday, April 23, 1998

Thursday's Child Has Far to Go…On Grace

I slept with Leiah last night. This morning there was a lot of blood in her diaper.

Today's plan was to move Leiah to a private room around noon and get her settled. Then at 1:30 p.m. we were to gather in her room to say goodbye, witness her ventilator being unhooked, and watch her quietly slip away. Although I knew this was the plan, I didn't believe it was going to happen.

Around 1:30, everyone arrived, psyched up for saying goodbye. There were lots of tears and Reverend Debbie Dennis said the *Ministry for the Dying*. Then, everyone except parents and medical staff left.

Although I said goodbye, I didn't mean it. I wasn't ready to let Leiah go.

Denial? Maybe, but it was denial mixed with intuition, because what happened next was unexpected.

The doctor bent over to examine Leiah. He lingered, straightened and turned. "I'm not sure what's happening," he began, "but Leiah is breathing above the ventilator."

We gasped.

"Not only that but since moving to this room, she has not had a seizure."

At first the words did not penetrate. When they did, I dared to dream. *Was this the miracle we'd been praying for? Was Leiah being spared, like Isaac, like Jairus' daughter?*

The doctor interrupted my silent queries.

"It is probably only temporary, but in view of what has happened, we will change the plan. We will observe Leiah for twenty-four hours, do another EEG, and meet again to discuss a new plan."

His tone was more grave than optimistic, but it didn't matter. It was a reprieve.

More importantly, it was grace.

Today is Anne Armstrong's birthday: Anne, who drove downtown despite the hour and with a headache, to sit with me when I was desperate and laden with guilt; Anne, who, from a place of love and compassion, assured me Leiah would be fine, in order to give each of us the hope we needed to survive another day; Anne, cheerleader for Leiah's modelling shows and impersonations; Anne, encourager extraordinaire, who assured an insecure Leiah that she was indeed special, very special.

Leiah to die on Anne's birthday? Preposterous! God and Leiah loved and honoured Anne too much to allow that. *Thursday* had changed to *Tuesday*: going from "far to go" to "full of grace" in homage to a woman who saved both daughter and mother from self-recrimination. This special Thursday proved that God's grace was in control.

Nevertheless, it was difficult for everyone to go home knowing we'd have to return the next day for "take two." David was very angry. He'd expected today to be *the* day. But it didn't feel right to me, and apparently not to Leiah. I slept alone Thursday night.

***

Friday, April 24, 1998

Friday's Child Is Loving and Giving

I woke up with hope Friday, although the seizures had returned Thursday afternoon. After Friday morning's EEG, I was told there was no change in her condition and that we should continue as originally planned. David's mom was there when we heard the news. She put her arm around me and suggested we go downstairs for a coffee. As we walked I shared a dream I'd had of my three girls getting together to play cards when they were eighty-nine, eighty-three and eighty. As I spoke, the words caught in my throat. That's when I knew it wouldn't happen, that today would be *the* day. At that moment, Michael, the chaplain, approached. I met his eyes, whimpered, "I'm going to lose her," and collapsed into his arms.

At 1:30 p.m. I was sitting beside David in the parent room. After confirming the time on my watch, I told David, "It's time." We rose reluctantly and, eyes downcast, inched down the cold corridor. My legs felt like concrete blocks. I did not want to make this trip. The only control I had was the speed at which I travelled: I chose *slow*.

As we entered the room, the scene differed from yesterday. Leiah was still lying in bed, in the centre of the room, but there was a different nurse. She greeted us softly and continued her task, filling up syringes and placing them on a tray table near the window. The nurse explained that the syringes were filled with morphine and were there "just in case" Leiah became distressed when the respirator was disconnected. Reverend Debbie Dennis wasn't there today. She'd cleared her calendar yesterday, but couldn't return today. Michael, the chaplain, took her place. His tall, lanky frame leaned against the wall, near the door. Dr. Shemie entered, nodded respectfully, and explained the plan.

"I'm going to remove the respirator, then I will examine Leiah. The examination should reveal what is likely to happen." We watched as he disconnected lines and pulled the tube out of her mouth. It was a relief to see her face without a protruding tube. Then he bent over and listened to her heart with his stethoscope. After a minute, maybe less, he turned, looked at us, and quietly confirmed our fears, "She's not going to make it." Then he left us with her.

Circling the bed, our eyes darted back and forth between Leiah's face, chest, and the monitor, comparing what we witnessed on her body with what the monitor measured. The line on the monitor was falling and numbers were starting to diminish. Words caught in my throat. Fearing for time, I leaned over my daughter and managed to whimper that I loved her… that I'd see her in her sisters, that she would go on in them.

Tears were shed, words of love spoken, and then someone—I think it was Drew—looked up at the monitor. He said, "It's broken…get the nurse." We all looked up. The line was flat. We held our collective breaths. The nurse arrived, looked at Leiah, then the screen, and left the room.

Seconds later, Dr. Shemie arrived. After glancing at the monitor, he placed his stethoscope on my daughter's chest, listened, and slowly lifted it off.

For just that moment I still clung to a world where children recover from illness and flat lines on monitors meant equipment malfunction. All that changed with these two words, "She's gone."

The words were a sucker punch, unleashing a torrent of pain. Wailing her name in a primal cry, I crumpled, pulling David down with me. He strained to keep both of us upright. When he whispered, "My back," I realized I had a decision to make.

The moment Dr. Shemie told us Leiah was gone was a defining moment, a tearing away from everything I had known. It marked a separation of *before* and *after*. The first moment *after*, when David was straining to hold me up, was equally defining. I had a choice. I could either collapse to the floor, and risk putting David's back out, or choose to rise and soldier on. Almost everything in me wanted to crumble, but I chose differently. I dug deep, summoned an inner strength I didn't know I had, and pulled myself upright. Glimpsing my daughter's pale face and lightless eyes almost drove me down, but I steeled myself. Stifling a sob, I turned to the chaplain.

"Could you please say something?" I whispered.

I can't recall what he said but I know his voice boomed with passion and conviction, and a tone that suggested a raised fist at the source of this sorry scene. Perhaps it was Romans 8:38-39:

> *For I am convinced that neither death nor life, neither angels nor demons, neither the present nor the future, nor any powers, neither height nor depth, nor anything else in all creation, will be able to separate us from the love of God that is in Christ Jesus our Lord.* (Romans 8:38-39)

After a while people started leaving, but the nurse and I stayed with Leiah's body. The nurse (Laureen, I think) told us we could stay as long as we needed. Together, we washed Leiah's matted hair, pulled it smoothly into a ponytail and braided it.

It was a holy, peace-filled time amid resignation.

Eventually I left my daughter's side. My father-in-law invited us all—family from both sides—out to dinner. Walking to the restaurant, I felt weak, empty and lost.

I'd been tied to Leiah for fourteen-and-a-half years, and these past six weeks had bonded us together as if with Krazy Glue. The warning on Krazy Glue reads: "DO NOT PULL APART. Krazy Glue® creates a VERY strong bond that's nearly impossible to break by pulling straight up and down." It doesn't say what happens if you do attempt to pull the pieces apart, but I'll tell you what happened to me. When Leiah's spirit rose, it ripped off a piece of mine, leaving an invisible yet gaping wound. I felt dessicated, an empty shell whose limbs moved only by reflex. Each step away from her hospital room felt like moving away from any semblance of strength as if I was Superman approaching kryptonite, sapping what little energy remained. Into that emptiness crept a thought: *Why not step into traffic and end this agony?* I couldn't imagine living with this feeling of emptiness and loss another minute, much less days, weeks, months, and years.

As my foot prepared to step off the curb, another thought occurred. *If I died, my mother would have to bear the pain I now feel.* I couldn't do that to her. I couldn't be responsible for causing this kind of pain to anyone else. So I steeled myself, pretended I was okay, and soldiered on to dinner.

After the meal, David and I returned to the hospital to pack our bags. I peeked in at Leiah one more time, but didn't enter the room. Perhaps I feared if I'd done so I might not be able to leave. Earlier that day David had booked a hotel room so we wouldn't have to drive home to Mississauga. We needed one more night of escape before returning to our new reality. As I climbed into bed that night, I wondered where Leiah was. I also wondered if there really was a God, and a life after death. I didn't understand why the Abraham-Isaac story hadn't worked out for us. *Why had Norm and Des said it was my story?* In the midst of overwhelming pain, my faith was floundering. I took my watch off and put it on the bedside table. As I did, I noticed something odd. The small hour hand was on the right side of the watch face. *Shouldn't it be on the left, near ten?* I peered closer. *The small hand is by the two and the long hand almost at the five.* I stared, waiting for the hands to move. They didn't. *I guess my battery died.* Then it hit me. *Wait a minute. Leiah died at 2:24. What did this mean? Could it be that when her spirit left her body, there was an electrical charge, one that affected my watch battery? Was this her way of letting me know she was still around?* Then I realized that Leiah had been born on a Friday at 2:24 p.m. and had died on a Friday at 2:24 p.m. *Born on a Friday in the flesh, born again in the spirit on a Friday…*

The hands on my watch, stuck at two and a little before five, were the sign I needed to carry me through the first night.

***

Saturday, April 25, 1998

Saturday's Child Works Hard For Its Living

David and I drove back to Mississauga on Saturday morning. Working on raw nerves, we went straight to Lee's Funeral Home. We hadn't called ahead. The morning was brisk and bright, and the street was quiet, not having woken up yet. Plucking up courage we walked through the large wooden doors. Just ahead was a large room, with one door partly open. It was filled with people in colourful garb and there was exotic music playing. Apparently a service was going on. A staff person approached us. We told her why we were there, and she led us into an office at the front of the building. We plunked ourselves down on leather chairs in front of a large, dark wooden desk. A short time later a forty-ish dark-haired man entered. Then we all set to work making plans we'd never imagined having to make.

We decided on Wednesday April 29 for the service, and worked backwards. There'd be two visitations on Tuesday, after body preparation on Monday. The death notice would go in the newspaper on Monday. But first, we had to word it. The man helped us with tough decisions like what to call her, and how to begin the death notice. Leiah's birth name was Vickery, Drew's surname. It was her legal name, but she'd used David's surname, Hampson, which I also used, in school. Many of her friends knew her only by Hampson. After consulting with Drew, we agreed to call her Leiah Vickery Hampson.

Wanting to recognize Leiah's strength and the fact she did not leave this world in pain, the funeral director suggested this wording, "Peacefully, after a courageous battle…" I wanted to conclude the notice with something profound but didn't feel capable of being deep that morning. The director offered a list of several options and I chose this one:

"The faithful departed are in God, the very heart of love. God has not taken them from us: He has hidden them in His Heart that they may be closer to ours."

As time went on I clung to that promise when it felt like I was losing my sense of Leiah. The sense of loss was a reminder to seek God's heart. Whenever I did, I found her.

After the plans were inked, we descended to the basement of the funeral home and entered a quiet room with a low ceiling. It was filled with caskets. I was immediately drawn to one in rich mahogany. After touching it I asked God and Leiah if it was the right one, and got the go ahead. Done. One choice I did not have to make was where to bury her. For that, I was grateful. A few weeks earlier, when I did not want to hear it, my mom and stepdad told me that *if* the worst happened, I could use their cemetery plot.

Our difficult duty done, we went home to start life as a family of four.

***

Sunday, April 26, 1998

Trinity Church, Streetsville burned down in the early hours of the morning. It was a sad day. The loss of the building elicited many memories. It was through Trinity's sturdy wooden doors that my three girls and I had entered three years earlier. It was in its sanctuary that I first felt the warmth of sunlight streaming through stained glass windows, warmth and light which helped me to absorb sermon messages I would need to navigate the coming week. It was in Trinity's baptismal font that my youngest daughter, Evann, was baptized. My faith had come alive in that building. So had Leiah's.

I recalled one Sunday morning, when twelve-year-old Leiah sat on a pew beside me. Upon hearing our rector [head priest] announce plans to demolish portions of the building in order to enlarge it, she pointed to the arch and asked, "What about that? Are they going to keep the arch in the new church?" A white proscenium arch covered the altar area and proclaimed in gold lettering, "This is none other than the house of God". The words come from Genesis 28:17 and the verse reads: "*He was afraid and said, 'How awesome is this place! This is none other than the house of God; this is the gate of heaven.'*" A bit surprised that a pre-teen with little church experience had an opinion about such a thing, I replied, "I don't know. I hope so." [*I now consider Leiah's question to be prophetic, evidence of a special spiritual connection that allowed her to recognize the importance of proclaiming whose house we were in, so that all who enter were reminded to check their pride at the door.*]

My sadness about losing the church building was, of course, eclipsed by the loss of Leiah. She was flesh, blood and spirit, not a brick-and-mortar container for memories. Nevertheless it was a difficult time for all of us who called Trinity our church home, and the fact that clergy, staff, and fellow church members stepped away from their own grief to rally around our family to support us through that time is a testament to the loving sacrifice to which we are all called, to bear one another's burdens.

My undying gratitude extends to all those who contributed in a host of ways: prayer, hospital visits, gifts, meals, organizing, officiating, serving, and performing musically at the service, the funeral tea, financial contributions, child care for my other two daughters, and all the heartfelt calls and letters. It was and continues to be touching and soul enlivening.

Monday, April 27, 1998

The day after the fire Reverend Debbie Dennis came to our house to help plan the funeral service. I told her about my watch stopping, and Leiah's story *My Guardian Angel,* and that I was starting to wonder if somehow, some way, Leiah knew her life would be short. I was beginning to wrestle with the idea that perhaps this was all part of God's plan. I wasn't happy about His plan, but who was I to argue with God? It actually gave me a measure of peace to believe Leiah's death was His will. After Debbie left I wrangled with the concept of miracles, and God's ways not being our ways. This was before I knew the verse that says,

> *"For my thoughts are not your thoughts, neither are your ways my ways," declares the Lord. "As the heavens are higher than the earth, so are my ways higher than your ways and my thoughts than your thoughts."* (Isaiah 55:8-9).

I went to my computer screen, and what flowed from my fingertips was "About Miracles," a message which was printed on the back of Leiah's *Service of Thanksgiving*, as well as in her high school yearbook, and other publications:

About Miracles

A lot of people have been praying for a miracle
   That despite all odds, Leiah would survive
   And we all would have another chance
   To be better parents, aunts, uncles, sisters, cousins and friends.

   Miracles are funny things; they're not always what they seem...
   Sort of like praying for one thing and getting another.
   We feel like saying, "I'm sorry God. You got it wrong; I didn't ask for THAT."

   Well, God's ways are not ours. I take comfort in believing that
   The more the ways of this world make sense to us

The further away we are from what really makes sense.

I believe that a lot of miracles have occurred over the past several weeks.
I'm certain that despite the physical manifestations of Leiah's disease
She felt at peace inside.
Although she could not speak to us
Her spirit did hear all the loving words
Feel all the caring touches
And gloried in the many heartfelt prayers.

Leiah was a gift to us, one we neither deserved nor paid for
She was never ours to own, only ours to care for and enjoy.

As a mother my wish is that Leiah's legacy would be this:
That all parents ensure that their children know they are cherished
Beyond any job, material possession or other distraction
So that every night each child can go to bed knowing how much he or she is loved
In spite of any disagreements or harsh words that might have preceded bedtime
So that if that day were to be their last
That child would be able to say he or she felt loved.

Because that's all that really matters.

***

Tuesday, April 28, 1998

Tuesday's Child is Full of Grace - Visitation Day

The support we received was immense, but the experience was still exhausting. I remember snippets: my Aunt Joan pinning a crystal angel on my sweater (which I wore daily for years until it slipped off one day, leaving me bereft); the nurse who was there when Leiah died; the many parents who said they "couldn't imagine"; friends of Leiah's who couldn't understand; neighbours, extended family, friends, church members, colleagues from so many intersecting walks of our collective lives. I remember stepping away briefly with two women from Community Bible Study who said Leiah's death would bring many to faith.

At the time I thought, yes, there will be hundreds at the funeral where seeds of faith might be planted but in 2014, those women's words again came to mind. I wondered if there was a greater import to them, that perhaps telling Leiah's story now, sixteen years later, might move even more to believe.

Leiah's casket was closed. I felt it was too personal a sight for sharing. Yet, she did look beautiful. She wore her grade eight graduation dress—the slinky dark blue sheath with light blue and white daisies. A white baby blanket her Grandma McGill had knit was draped over her shoulders as a shawl. On her pinky finger was a sapphire birthstone ring, given to her by her Grandma Vickery, who shared a September birthday. On her ring finger was the wedding band her father had given to me. Around her neck was a necklace with praying hands on the outside, and her name engraved on the inside—a baptismal gift from her Grandpa Leavens. Her hair was a cascade of soft waves and her makeup was natural-looking, her lips a dreamy shade of coral. Her lipstick was the only thing that gave me pause. Leiah tended to favour rosy colours for her lips. However, my enduring memory is one of beauty and peace.

But when the lid was lifted and I saw her body for the first time in four days, I was devastated. It hurled me back to the moment of loss all over again. If I had allowed those feelings to overtake me a moment longer, I might not have been able to recover. Although part of me wanted to tarry with my daughter's shell, I feared what would happen if I stayed too long. *Could the four-day buffer between then and now compress to nothing? Would I have to start anew?* Drew chose to linger. I stepped away.

Mark North, whom Leiah had assisted in *Sonshine Land,* Trinity's pre-school class, visited but we didn't connect that day. He later wrote:

"To be honest, you were constantly surrounded and I couldn't summon up the courage to talk to you. Believe it or not, Leiah is the first person who I've known that's died. Saying 'I'm sorry' seemed like such a hollow sentiment but I didn't want you to think that my heart, prayers, and thoughts were not with you that day. I hope this doesn't sound strange but when I was at the funeral home and everyone's head was hanging, I prayed in front of Leiah's casket and it suddenly dawned on me that the light in heaven just grew brighter…I thought Leiah was special too."

That is something I *want* to remember about the visitation.

***

Wednesday, April 29, 1998
Wednesday's Child is Full of Woe
The funeral. Trinity Streetsville had burned down, but since it had been under renovation, the service couldn't have been

held there anyway. The pastor at nearby Mississauga Gospel Temple [now known as Portico] graciously offered his church, which was big enough to accommodate a crowd. Over four hundred came.

Reverend Debbie Dennis and Reverend Michael Marshall (the chaplain from Sick Kids Hospital) officiated. Scriptures included Psalm 23, 1 Corinthians 15:51-57, and John 20:10-18.

> *Listen, I tell you a mystery: We will not all sleep, but we will all be changed—in a flash, in the twinkling of an eye, at the last trumpet. For the trumpet will sound, the dead will be raised imperishable, and we will be changed. For the perishable must clothe itself with the imperishable, and the mortal with immortality. When the perishable has been clothed with the imperishable, and the mortal with immortality, then the saying that is written will come true: "Death has been swallowed up in victory." "Where, O death, is your victory? Where, O death, is your sting?" The sting of death is sin, and the power of sin is the law. But thanks be to God! He gives us the victory through our Lord Jesus Christ* (1 Corinthians 15:51-57).

Songs included, "Pie Jesu," "On Eagle's Wings," "Abba! Father!" "Praise My Soul, The King of Heaven," "There is a Redeemer," "Here is Love," "Be Still," "Purify my Heart," "Now We Remain," and my request, "Amazing Grace." Speakers included family members from all sides.

I was numb throughout much of the service. I only remember tidbits, like Debbie Dennis' memory of Leiah tottering down the church aisle in high heels, and Anna's reflections about Leiah's love of children, stickers and architecture. I also remember John and Judith MacDonald's rendition of "Pie Jesu," and singing my heart out during "Amazing Grace."

Family members had to leave right after the service to go to the cemetery and by the time we returned many people had left. Had I been thinking clearly I would have planned it differently, but I wasn't thinking clearly.

Part 6
the beginning of *after*

Gifts
left behind

A reporter from the *Toronto Sun* interviewed me for a possible Mother's Day story. After sharing details with her, she told me her editor would probably deem it "too sad a story for Mother's Day." I must have taken her comments as a challenge because after she left I climbed the stairs, plunked myself down in front of the computer, and began to write:

"Some might think this is too sad a story to read on Mother's Day, a day that's supposed to be for breakfast in bed, handpicked dandelions and homemade cards. But it's not an entirely sad story. True, it's the story of a mom who buried her fourteen-year-old daughter eleven days ago after a short and sudden illness. But it's the story of so much more—perhaps even what it means to be a mom."

I wrote about the lead-up to Leiah's illness, included some hospital scenes, and called the six weeks I spent at *Sick Kids* Hospital "*exhausting*" but a "*mother's joy.*" In the process of writing, I realized that I had cherished the opportunity to spend time at Leiah's bedside, "*away from the distractions of life that too often keep one away from what's really important.*" In caring for Leiah, I wrote, "*she was my baby again.*"

The piece included the fact that my watch had stopped when she died, and that she died on the same day of the week and at the same time that she was born. I ended the article with a reference to Leiah's *My Guardian Angel* story and wrote: "*That is my daughter's Mother's Day gift to me.*"

There were many other gifts that I found once I started looking.

A few days later, when I was home alone, I ventured into Leiah's room. After lifting the corner of a Leonardo DiCaprio poster, I discovered she'd written "I [heart symbol] J" directly on the wall. I wondered who J was. Moving to her closet I sat on the floor, and settled in for a long time of sorting.

I found her diary first. Daring to open it, despite an admonition on the cover not to do so, I quickly closed it after reading the first couple of lines, which even more clearly expressed how she felt about anyone who might be reading her private words. There were many papers in her closet—mostly school work. After sifting through mounds of paper, I came upon a pencil sketch on a piece of lined notebook paper. It was a picture of Leiah and her sisters. Each sister had bangs with long hair, and was similarly attired in a sleeveless shirt with a peace symbol on it. Leiah printed each of their names and ages above each figure. Each girl's arms were bent upward, with their thumbs raised in a "thumbs up" pose. At the top of the page Leiah wrote "Do not throw out." The admonition was clearly for me not to throw this piece of art out in a cleaning spree. Leiah obviously wanted this picture preserved. *Had she known it would be the last sketch of all three sisters at the ages they were when she died?*

There was another gift in her closet: a rolled up piece of artwork. When I unfurled it I discovered a watercolour Leiah had painted of an angelic being, wearing a long, flowing purple robe, and lying on a cloud. The "angel" had long, brown hair, and blue eyes, and above her were scales. At the bottom of the picture were green trees and hills. I wondered: *was this some sort of vision she'd had?*

I also received from one of Leiah's teachers a piece of pottery she'd fashioned in art class. It was a pink ceramic dog with purple wings. *Was this something she'd dreamed of?*

These gifts fascinated me. *Were they proof of an otherworldly connection? Had she known her death was imminent?*

Despite the spiritual highs from these discoveries, the reality that I was a human mother grieving the loss of my daughter kept pulling at me. I was always tired. Weekday mornings I would walk Torey and Evann to the bus stop, then go home to sleep. Most days I woke up in time to meet Evann when the bus dropped her off after morning kindergarten. Sometimes I did not. On those days the bus returned to the school with Evann on it. My alarm clock was sometimes the telephone ringing and then the school secretary saying, "No one was at the bus stop to meet Evann, so she's here at school. Please come to pick her up."

Left to my own devices, I might have just slept and hung out in Leiah's room during most of my waking hours, but two daughters and a husband didn't allow for that. I had to keep moving. I didn't write much in my diary during that time.

David and I didn't mourn Leiah's loss the same way, but I didn't realize it at the time. Fifteen years later, in 2013, when I wrote to Reverend Debbie Dennis to tell her I was thinking of writing a book about Leiah, I asked her what she remembered. She wrote:

"I remember the time of Leiah's illness and death as a sad one. I remember how difficult it was for you and your family and how everyone dealt with it differently."

She was right. After Leiah died, I kept a lot to myself. David was more expressive. He said he couldn't handle walking up the stairs and seeing Leiah's room every day, that it was too painful. He wanted to sell the house and start fresh. I didn't have the strength to fight him about it, so I agreed, although I didn't realize what I'd be losing.

It meant packing up her room, and painting over "I *heart* J" and other scribblings in order to create a neutral palette for prospective buyers. Covering the marks she'd made was like losing another piece of her. Leaving the house also meant I couldn't go back into her room to just sit and remember.

David decided it would be a good idea to get away, so we flew out west to visit his best friend in Calgary, and rented a car to drive to B.C. I couldn't feel terribly happy about anything and I wondered about the point of the trip, but I can't fault David for trying to fix things. The trouble was that it wasn't fixable.

The house sold quickly and we bought a new one that had been built, but not finished on the inside. We were able to choose flooring and cupboards, but I had very little interest in the process.

When it came time to sign the papers we met with a real estate lawyer our realtor had recommended. The lawyer, Betty, asked why we were moving after only two-and-a-half years. After an uncomfortable silence, we told her. When I mentioned that I had simply packed all of Leiah's things into boxes because I didn't have the strength to sort through them or get rid of anything, Betty looked pensive, then spoke, "All of my daughter's things are still in boxes in my basement and it's been ten years."

I was shocked. I had felt alone—as if no one else could know what it was like to lose a child. Now we were sitting across from someone who knew. Although I had doubted the wisdom of selling the house so soon after Leiah's death, I interpreted this meeting as a sign we were on the right track, or at least that God knew we desperately needed encouragement and provided it. Betty said something else that day. Some might have considered it a platitude, but I found it comforting. As we stood up to leave, she quietly said, "Sometimes God needs another flower for his garden."

Recently, while Googling the name Leiah, I was floored to discover that in Hawaiian, Leiah means "heavenly flower." Had Betty known?

Within seven months of Leiah's death I suffered two more losses. The first was five days later. On the day we buried Leiah, my step-grandmother, whom I called Aunt Gladys, died. A few weeks later I noticed something amiss with my father. One morning he called from his apartment in east Mississauga to say he was on his way over to visit me in west Mississauga. A trip that should have taken twenty-five minutes took an hour and a half. When I asked what took him so long he wasn't sure. Somehow he'd driven forty-five minutes north to Caledon before turning around.

When he'd visited Leiah at Sick Kids Hospital I'd noticed my father's limbs were scrawny while his stomach was larger than ever, but since I was preoccupied with Leiah, the information hadn't fully registered. When Dad finally went to his doctor, he was immediately referred to a specialist who diagnosed hepatic encephalopathy, a loss of brain function that occurs when the liver is unable to remove toxins from the blood. Dad went downhill quickly. I took turns with his fiancée and my siblings sitting vigil at his bedside for seven days in November after he slipped into a coma. He passed away on November 8, 1998, only six-and-a-half months after Leiah.

Debbie Dennis, who had supported us throughout Leiah's illness and had conducted the funeral service, left Trinity to go to another church at the end of June 1998, but kept in touch with us. When I met with her at the end of the year and told her what had happened since, she asked, "Are you beginning to feel like Job yet?"

It took me years to appreciate the story of Job, but when I did, I felt honoured that God might test my faith as he did with Job. In the Bible story, the turning point for Job comes when Job realizes he can't possibly understand all God is, knows and does. God is in charge whereas Job, you and I are the worker bees given tasks to complete on a "need to know" basis. In the Bible, after Job acknowledges all God is, Job repents and intercedes for his friends who had misrepresented God's intent for allowing Job's suffering. After Job repents and prays for his friends, God blesses Job by giving him double what he had had before.

I used to wonder whether Job was comforted by his new children, knowing he had to lose the originals to get the new ones, but I suppose that's the whole point. If you lose someone—for reasons we may never fully understand here on earth—then you know the pain of having a hole inside of you. When someone comes along to fill that gap—be it a person, or a more vibrant connection with God—you are in a position to recognize and appreciate the blessings all the more.

I came to appreciate Job's experience in a new way in early summer 2014 after we were shaken by the death of a young family member. In the wee hours of one morning, I awoke and sensed a presence with me, one of unlimited power and possibilities. The experience left me believing in and trusting in God's sovereign power even more. It also made me realize that nothing is impossible with God. If something is His will and your prayers align with it, it's as good as done. It also made me realize there's no point in doing things your own way, because He'll steamroll over it if it's not part of His plan. At that moment, the following passage came alive for me:

> *Then Job replied to the LORD: "I know that you can do all things; no purpose of yours can be thwarted.*
>
> *You asked, 'Who is this that obscures my plans without knowledge?'*
>
> *Surely I spoke of things I did not understand, things too wonderful for me to know.*
>
> *"You said, 'Listen now, and I will speak; I will question you, and you shall answer me.'*
>
> *My ears had heard of you but now my eyes have seen you.*
>
> *Therefore I despise myself and repent in dust and ashes."* (Job 42:1-6)

The

why

When I was struggling with "why" Leiah had died, I tormented myself, wondering if there was anything I could have done to prevent Leiah's illness. Someone told me "the die had been cast." I don't know when that was—if it was set prior to her birth, if a specific event cast it, or if there was a point of no return—and I won't know for sure until heaven. For now, that is enough.

We do have some answers. We received autopsy results about six months after Leiah's death. The autopsy listed her cause of death as "sepsis." Sepsis occurs when chemicals are released into the bloodstream to fight an infection that has triggered inflammation throughout the body. Such inflammation can set off a cascade of changes that can damage multiple organ systems, causing them to fail. That does describe what I saw.

When she was in hospital, although viral encephalitis was mentioned, Leiah's doctor kept talking about "sustained status epilepticus." I spent time researching many of the terms the doctors had mentioned, although I didn't always note my sources. Somewhere I read the following about "non-convulsive status epilepticus": patients appear forgetful and sleepy, behave like they're deaf, blind or drugged, show poor motor control, abnormal balance and may fall frequently. This describes so clearly what I witnessed two to three days before Leiah's first seizure. *Had I only known then what I know now…*

Of Prisms
and piñatas

Recently I had a vision of Leiah as a crystal prism—stunning and precious, dancing in the light, refracting colours. Then I saw the prism smashing. It was heartbreaking. No more dancing, no more light. But when I looked closer I discovered among the bits of broken glass hundreds of tiny prisms that had been locked inside. A consolation prize? Yes. But a prize nonetheless. The hundreds of tiny prisms contained many miracles.

During the course of Leiah's illness, when so many disparate people were forced together to support Leiah and each other, old grievances had to be pushed aside. I even shared a room with my ex-husband for six weeks! There were many miracles of healing (relationships), strength (Leiah's), and grace (being given one more day with her).

I also thought about piñatas. My sister, Nichole, has two daughters, Katia, ten, and Isla, seven. (One of Isla's middle names is Lea, a nod to her late cousin.) One day, I emailed Nichole to ask whether Katia and Isla would want a piñata at their birthday party. Nichole wrote back, "They would upset Katia. We have neighbours who would have piñata parties where older boys would come and beat up Dora and other cute cartoon animals. This would traumatize poor Katia. I've never understood why they don't make piñatas representing evil characters. This makes much more sense to me than bashing Winnie the Pooh in the head."

Maybe piñatas were also part of Leiah's divination. Maybe, like Jesus, she became like poor Dora in piñata form. The seizures were like the older boys' bats, bashing Leiah's stuffing out and breaking her body. Yet when it was finished—when her outer shell was completely broken—many treasures were left behind.

Sharon remembers this about Leiah's final birthday party:

"Only a few people took a swing before the piñata burst, sending candy flying everywhere. However, I had sneakily observed that because of the manner in which the piñata burst, a lot of candy was still in the remaining piece of piñata that had fallen on the ground. I tried to tell everyone, but in the scramble nobody listened, so I had a few more Cherry Blaster packs in my bag than others. It was good too, because I slept over that night, and Leiah and I ate most of it while watching movies that night and the next morning."

Although Sharon tried to tell the others about the treasure trove that remained, nobody listened. Their focus was on what was obvious, which they gathered and took with them. It was their loss, but Sharon's and Leiah's gain.

***

My going back to re-live Leiah's arrival, presence and departure from this world reminded me of many treasures I had hidden in my heart for the past sixteen years, treasures I wanted to share because they're way better than Cherry Blasters. They provide hope amid pain, and evidence of a plan in the midst of apparent chaos.

Recently I received two more gifts. My mother shared something she'd never told me. For some time after Leiah's death, my mother had wondered about something. Not everyone could fit comfortably in Leiah's room, so my mother had been in the anteroom the day Leiah died. It had bothered my mom a lot that she wasn't by her firstborn granddaughter's side when she died, and that perhaps Leiah hadn't known she was there. One day, months after Leiah died, my mom told me that she had heard a voice in her mind say, "I knew, Grandma."

A second great gift was to reconnect with Leiah's friend, Sharon. A gifted and confident woman who would have made an excellent doctor, Sharon chose to pursue law as a career. (I'm certain she is a wonderful lawyer.) When I sat down with Sharon on a lovely day in June 2014 at an outdoor café in Toronto, she told me that on Friday, April 24, 1998, sometime between two and three p.m., she had been walking home from school when suddenly she knew that Leiah was no longer on earth. When Sharon arrived home, her mother was waiting to give Sharon the news. Sharon told her, "I know."

Sometime later, Sharon had had what she described as a "different kind of dream." In it an ethereal-looking Leiah, dressed in her grade eight graduation dress, walked across a meadow towards Sharon. Leiah told her dear friend not to worry, that she was fine.

I shivered when Sharon told me about that dream. Leiah had been buried in her graduation dress, but only family knew this because we had chosen a closed casket. In Old English *Leah* means "meadow" and in Hawaiian, *Leiah* means "heavenly flower." Our heavenly flower had greeted Sharon in a meadow and, just as my friends Anne Armstrong and Des Torrie had told me, she was "fine."

***

An enduring picture I have of Leiah, both as a photograph and in my mind's eye, was taken atop Sulphur Mountain in Banff, Alberta. Leiah was almost six years old, and not yet a big sister. It was colder than we'd expected and we were not prepared. Leiah stood shivering in a royal blue spring coat as I snapped the photo. Her blue eyes were the deepest blue I'd ever seen them, reflecting off her coat.

It is those eyes I imagine looking into when she greets me on the other side of this mortal coil. I envision her approaching with grace and confidence, a cache of children on her shirttails. It is a reunion I patiently long for. When I look into her eyes I will feel known and loved. But most importantly, I will feel special, just like Leiah.

What I
learned about grief

1. Only a small percentage of people know the right thing to say at the right time, but most people mean well, so try to give them grace. Ironically, someone might say something one day that will sound horrible—hurtful in its emptiness—yet another day it will be just what you need to hear. The best kind of support comes from friends/family who make themselves available to simply *listen* and not to offer any advice or even their own stories, unless you ask them for it. *Listening* is one of the greatest gifts you can give to anyone in need of healing. Everyone needs to be able to tell their story. If you have an opportunity to listen to someone, restrain yourself from speaking and simply be fully present. Allowing someone to share openly and honestly about the myriad feelings he or she may have, without fear of judgment, is a gift. Grieving people might feel anger, sorrow, regret, frustration, guilt, fear or a host of other emotions. You feel what you feel. As Bruce, a friend of Drew's said to me sixteen years ago, "Don't let anyone 'should' on your feelings."

2. Grieving takes a lot of energy. Some experts estimate grief takes 70% of a person's energy, so expect to be tired. Don't try to do 100% of what you used to do. Leave wide margins in each day.

3. Acknowledge that every individual grieves differently. Your spouse and other family members may be in a totally different head and heart space. Respect each person's own way to grieve. Sometimes denial is the only thing that can get you through a day, week, month or more. Sometimes being busy is needed, sometimes just lying there doing nothing. It's all *mourning*— expressing your loss. Sometimes you won't have the energy to let the pain come out.

4. Finding meaning or a legacy for your loved one can be helpful, but if it doesn't happen right away, or if it doesn't seem to happen at all, don't beat yourself up about it. (It took me sixteen years to write this book!) His/her legacy can rest in the feelings evoked after he/she is gone.

5. In the midst of the pain, acknowledge it, then find gratitude for your loved one's presence in your life. Recognize that going through great suffering plants the seeds of compassion. One day you will be able to draw on that compassion to support others through their own trying times.

6. Writing honestly about one's feelings can be beneficial. A former executive director of Bereaved Families of Ontario/ Halton-Peel, Wendy Dean, journaled almost daily after losing her daughter Rachael. She described it as one way of trying to cope with the overwhelming pain and confusion of grieving. Dean went on to publish a book called *Journaling a Pathway Through Grief.* She wrote, "As a former mental health/psychiatric nurse, my clinical understanding of grief and knowledge of current grief theory did not adequately describe or explain my lived experience of grief. I used my

journal excerpts as a means of promoting a new understanding of grief through the lens of my actual experience and contemporary bereavement theories in *Journaling a Pathway through Grief*. The word *pathway* referred to my attempt to find my way through darkness and despair and make meaning from the experience so that I could go on living without bitterness. Thus, *pathway* was really a metaphor for the profound, mysterious, twisting back and forth subterranean journey or passage of grief, a necessary soul journey through darkness in order to get to the light."

Make your *pathway* however you can. If you're not a writer, then draw, paint, sing, talk, garden, walk, run, shoot hoops: do whatever it takes to get the pain out.

7. Don't compare yourself to others who are grieving. Some people visit or camp out at their child's grave daily; others go rarely, if ever. Do what works for you.

8. When you can't get away from thoughts, turn the television on. It's a wonderful escape. I will always be grateful to Kelsey Grammer's character *Frasier* for giving me my first hearty laugh after Leiah died.

9. Be prepared that when you go out shopping and see your loved one's favourite cereal, you may start crying. If you see someone from the back, whose body type, hair, and gait matches his/hers, you might not be able to move/speak. Don't be surprised if you're in line behind someone who's complaining about something trivial, and you have to hold back a compulsion to snap at them. Be prepared for not being prepared about everything that might trigger tears, anger or regret.

10. If you have lost a child, find other grieving parents with whom you can share your loss, but be protective about who you choose to share feelings and details. Remember, you're

vulnerable and weak. Not everyone is trustworthy or up to the task of bearing someone else's deep heartache. Bereaved Families of Ontario offers "Share and Support" nights, closed support groups, and initial meetings with another bereaved parent where you can tell your story. Not everyone is a "group" person, and it's important not to enter into the process too early when it may simply hurt too much to listen. But it can be helpful to hear other stories. At the very least, you know you are not alone.

11. There are different kinds of grief support groups. Funeral homes, Bereaved Families of Ontario, and the Coping Centre are a few examples. There is also counselling. If you can't afford counselling, non-profit agencies often offer services on a sliding scale fee, and may have free sessions available at certain times. If you're someone who dislikes all types of counselling, try sports. Maybe by the 14th hole or third quarter you'll be ready to share a little.

12. Find what works for you. After Leiah died, I was starving for hope and found it helpful to do a lot of reading of stories where people had a sense of an afterlife.

13. The minister who did my daughter's funeral recommended a book called "Praying our Goodbyes" by Joyce Rupp. It analyzes what a goodbye is, "an empty place in us ... a space that cries out to be filled," and includes exercises at the end of each chapter. It's not just about death; it's about all the goodbyes we face in life.

14. Be aware that once we've experienced great grief, all further losses have the potential to reopen that wound.

15. If you've got the energy, and you're an "expressive" type, organizing a fundraiser event is an option. (Personally I think it's a lot of work, and wonder if the money is commensurate with the work/energy/expenses required, but

it can help some people in their grief journey, while making a difference financially as well as increasing awareness about particular diseases/conditions). It's also an opportunity for others to remember your loved one and gather around to support you.

16. We never get "closure" from grief. It bubbles up whenever it needs to. I look at my loss as life *before* and life *after*. Life was simpler and I was more naïve before Leiah died. Whenever I want to remember that simpler time—when life carried on as expected—I go back to the house we lived in before the one where Leiah got sick. So far I haven't knocked on the door; I just park across the street, look at it, and remember. It's like taking a vacation from reality, and when I leave, it's like flying from the South Seas back to harsher climes.

17. In order to make good of something bad, you have to give back…when you have the strength to do so. Otherwise you risk getting stuck inside with all the hurt. That's why I volunteered with Bereaved Families of Ontario/Halton-Peel for many years; that's why I joined the team of the Streetsville COPING program; and that's why I became a Stephen Minister, someone who walks alongside someone going through a life challenge. I want to turn my hurts into healing.

18. Take time to be still. Recently someone told me she'd misplaced her keys and realized she needed to return to the place she'd lost them in an attempt to find them. Mourning well is a little like that. You need to go back to where you got stuck and ask for help to find your way out.

After Leiah died, talking with other bereaved parents and joining a moms' support group was a life preserver. When I finished my group, I wanted to give back. Despite a recommendation to wait a couple of years, I talked an organization into letting me train as a volunteer facilitator only sixteen months after Leiah's death. I picked up a lot of useful information and threw myself into volunteering with them, reasoning that had Leiah survived with major disabilities, caring for her would have been my life. Hence I'd been given the gift of time and I should use the time I had to do good works.

I'm sure I helped a lot of people, but hope I didn't hurt any—because I wasn't ready. Learning things, keeping the information in your brain, and sharing it with others is one thing; letting it seep into your heart and pouring it out into other hearts is something completely different. Being present for someone in pain requires focus, patience, energy and empathy. I wasn't always fully present. With the exception of those whose loved ones had died by homicide or suicide, I thought others should "get" that this is all about God's will, so they should carry on and turn their losses into something good. I tried turning that lesson into a crash course, but it's a lesson that takes as long as it needs to take.

One day, about ten years after Leiah died, I was alone at home. I started to go through photos of Leiah and was suddenly overcome by how much I missed her. I remembered things she had said and did and how I felt when she was still here. The pain was unbearable. I felt myself sinking into a dark hole, deeper and deeper, desperate and desolate. I was frightened, and no one was there to help me out of it. Later I called my mom and told her what happened. She said, "Laura, I don't think you ever really grieved."

Was she right? Had I cut my mourning short? Had I actually run from the pain with all the volunteering? Was all that busy-ness an addiction? An escape from reality? Had I done all those "good works" to avoid feeling and facing the pain?

I recently met a woman whose daughter specializes in wound care. Shortly afterward, I met a nurse who does the same. I imagine the first thing that a wound specialist insists on is that the patient sit still so they can examine the wound and determine how best to care for it. Some wounds might do better with fresh air, others by being covered; some need ointment, and others stitching. But before a wound can be tended, the patient needs to be still so that the healer knows what she is dealing with.

I ran too many times for far too long. I'm finally being still, so that Great Physician can examine me and let me heal.

Epilogue

The new normal

The old adage that a picture is worth a thousand words rings true in the logo for *Bereaved Families of Ontario*, a mutual aid organization for grieving people. The top half of the logo contains three figures. In the middle is a tall male, on the right, a tall female, and on the left, a short female, presumably a child. Each figure is holding hands with the person nearest. The figures cast shadows on the bottom half of the logo, below a dark line meant to represent the ground. Among the shadows, however, are four figures, not three. The fourth is a little taller than the short female and is shaped like a male. The inference is that a fourth figure exists, although now invisibly.

After Leiah died, when the four of us—David, Torey, Evann and I—entered a room, others saw four people, but we knew Leiah's shadow was also there. Our first trip to a restaurant was jarring. When the hostess asked, "How many?" the sound "f" caught in my throat. I imagine it was the same for David. Eventually one of us managed to whisper "Four," and a perplexed hostess led us to a square table with four chairs. I looked longingly at the larger round table where we'd sat in the past.

Our new home had three bedrooms, one each for Torey and Evann, and a master bedroom with adjoining office. We hung photos of Leiah on the walls, alongside those of her sisters, but all of Leiah's things were neatly packed away in boxes in the basement. I felt comfort looking at the photos, but David did not.

David and I grieved Leiah's loss very differently. Although we went as a couple to speak with two other couples whose children had died—one at Bereaved Families of Ontario/ Halton-Peel, and one at The Coping Centre in Cambridge, Ontario—David and I joined separate support groups. Mine was for mothers only while David joined a mixed group. Torey and Evann went to children's groups led by a psychologist, where they could draw and paint to express their feelings. I kept in touch with several members from my moms' group for many years, before eventually drifting apart.

I stayed home for a year-and-a-half after Leiah died, before returning to work part-time at first and eventually full-time. I started a new career as a Communications Coordinator at the local mental health association in November 2000. Today I do contract work and write when I can.

David and I separated five years later. David remarried in 2008 while I married Michael in December 2011.

Torey is currently living in Halifax, Nova Scotia, where she stopped after riding her bicycle across the country in 2013. Evann is going to university and working part-time. She lives with Michael and me in Mississauga. Torey and Evann remember their sister on their arms. The letters "LVE" (for Leiah, Victoria—Torey's given name—and Evann) are tattooed on Torey's left inner wrist, while a hair bow along with the letters "LVE" are tattooed on Evann's upper left arm. Evann says she cannot remember her big sister, but honours a memory we told her about: one day Leiah spent more than an hour painstakingly inserting hairclips and barrettes into Evann's hair, in an attempt to make her mane the craziest on "Crazy Hair Day." The letters of the girls' tattoos proclaim that they are three, not two sisters, and they also hint at "LIVE" and "LOVE," bereft only of a vowel.

***

A week before I finished the first draft of this book, something remarkable happened. For sixteen years I'd struggled with the Biblical story of Abraham and Isaac, the story Norm and Des had said was God's message for me.

The first weekend in June is Streetsville's Bread and Honey Festival. On the Sunday morning of Bread and Honey weekend, there is always a road race which requires road closures. Every year on Bread and Honey Festival weekend, I head out to church, forgetting that it is Bread and Honey weekend. This year was no exception. It took four different tries and then a one-kilometre hike to get to Trinity Streetsville, my home church. My husband and I trekked in, a half-hour late, yet just in time for the Bible reading: it was Genesis 22, Abraham's sacrifice of Isaac.

My heart was in my throat as I had just been writing about that story days earlier. I settled in to hear what the guest preacher, Reverend Kyle Hackmann, had to say about the passage.

God was testing Abraham, he said, but not by holding out a bar and asking, "Can you jump this high?" Instead, as He does for each of us, God gave Abraham tests so that when doubts and worries came to the surface, Abraham could do business with them and become strengthened.

Kyle said, "That which is buried deep inside rises." That was how I had studied when I was a child. I had enjoyed tests. I just went in, concentrated on the question, and waited for the knowledge to rise. Trouble came when the knowledge wasn't there to rise—when I'd missed a lesson due to illness, or when a concept was beyond my ken. (I felt the latter way a lot in high school Math, Science and Geography classes.) But if the answer was there—even if it was buried deeply—it was exhilarating to feel it rise to the top and watch it flow out in my answers.

I liked the pastor's analogy but it started getting harder to listen to what else he had to say. "When God tests us, He'll push us to the edge, to get our complete attention and undivided loyalty." I thought about the edges I had had to go to with Leiah and grew more contemplative. Kyle continued, adding historical context, "Sadly, at the time, it was common for the firstborn to be sacrificed." The Bible says, "*The first offspring of every womb belongs to me*" (Exodus 34:19) and:

> *...all the first-born are mine. When I struck down all the firstborn in Egypt, I set apart for myself every firstborn in Israel, whether human or animal. They are to be mine. I am the Lord.* (Numbers 3:13)

Leiah was my firstborn. I am also a firstborn.

Pastor Kyle continued. "When you lose everything you *need* most, and it feels like God is calling you into the unknown, trust Him. He pushes you to the point where you won't give him what you hold back, but He wants your 'everything' and is willing to test you to get it." *Was this guy reading my mind?*

Two chapters earlier, Kyle reminded us, Abraham had been at a low point in his faith life. Now Abraham was at a high point. *Like my life: there were so many low points before the tests.*

Abraham hears the call of God and is diligent to obey Him, even rising early to start this difficult journey. How can Abraham do so? He is confident that God will provide what is needed.

Abraham does as he is told. He binds his son to the altar, arranges wood on it, reaches for a knife and is about to slaughter Isaac. Why? Because Abraham took God at His word. Although God's command was perplexing, and although He demanded everything Abraham held dear, Abraham didn't delay. Instead he trusted God and was prepared to give everything away. *As I was...although I did delay...*

Mount Moriah, Kyle said, is mentioned in only two places in the Bible: in Genesis 22 and 2 Chronicles. In 2 Chronicles 3, Mount Moriah is the place where the Lord provides:

> *Then Solomon began to build the temple of the LORD in Jerusalem on Mount Moriah, where the LORD had appeared to his father David. It was on the threshing floor of Araunah the Jebusite, the place provided by David.* (2 Chronicles 3:1)

As Kyle reflected on the father-son bonding experience provided by a three-day's journey up a mountain, I thought back to my own six-week journey alongside Leiah, and how tightly bound we had grown. When Kyle said, "Isaac was a very important child," I thought, *So was Leiah.*

In the Biblical account, the angel of the Lord rescued father and son in the nick of time, telling Abraham not to lay a hand on the boy. Abraham looked, saw a ram in a thicket waiting to take Isaac's place as a sacrifice, and released his son. Kyle drew parallels between Abraham and another man who was commanded by his father to pile wood on his back, wear a crown of thorns, and be obedient to the point of death. The man was Jesus. Kyle likened Jesus' situation to Abraham and Isaac's, suggesting it was as though Jesus' Father lifted a knife against Him, yet He stayed, willingly, trusting that His Father would provide.

I started to cry silently. Before hearing this sermon, I'd had an inkling of what Abraham had gone through, but now I was identifying with God. Frankly it was too much to absorb. I felt like I was drowning in the magnitude of what God had done for all of us, how horrific it must have been to raise His arm against His very Son and to carry through with His death, all for our sake. It was so overwhelming that I had to make a choice: I could either succumb and collapse, or shake the feeling off. I chose the latter and returned my attention to Kyle's summation of the true cost of faith. "God asks us to give him everything, yet we can do so trusting in His promise to provide what we need, knowing that obedience leads to an experience of God's blessings."

My Abraham/Isaac experience made it clear to me that these words were true. God does ask us for everything. Saying yes is not easy but He does provide what we need. And if we obey, we experience God's blessings. I've been there. Many times.

Later I thought about the story some more. *Maybe it was my story after all. Although it looked like God hadn't provided a ram to sacrifice in place of my child, He actually had. I hadn't seen the ram when I stood over Leiah's bed in that hospital room, because I was focused on what I was losing, her bodily presence. But that doesn't mean the ram wasn't there. The ram was Jesus, and although I couldn't see Him, He was also in the room, waiting to step in at the moment Leiah's heart stopped, to join His spirit with hers so that she would not have to face death alone. Leiah **had** been spared by Jesus—the "nice man" she had told me was in the story she'd written. He had indeed come to save her.*

It took sixteen years (and an inspired sermon) for me to realize that. It was finally time to leave Mount Moriah, confident in the knowledge that Leiah's life had indeed been spared.

A week later I heard another sermon. Newly ordained deacon Simon Davis preached about the Old Testament story of Jacob and Leah. When he said that "God opened Leah's womb because she felt like nobody loved her," I was dumbstruck. Leah, heavily veiled, had been given as a wife to Jacob by her father who knew Jacob loved her younger sister, Rachel. When God saw that Leah was unloved, He opened her womb, and gave her children—seven of them, one of whom, Judah, was a forefather of Jesus.

I recalled that long ago evening in January 1983 when I had received a precious gift from God, just as thousands of years ago, the biblical Leah had. On a day that each of us—Leah and I—had felt unloved by our husbands, God had opened each of our wombs. Leah had received her firstborn son, Reuben, and I, my firstborn daughter, Leiah.

Someone who had heard me tell Leiah's story had commented that it sounded like Leiah had come to save me. Leiah had indeed saved me, over and over again in life, and after she died, because she left behind gifts that I found when I needed them.

It took sixteen years to realize that the Abraham and Isaac story was indeed mine, to know in my spirit that God was faithful and that He had provided a ram sacrifice. I won't understand everything until I'm up there with Leiah, but that's okay.

Good things come to those who wait.

I can wait.

about the author

Laura Leavens is the mother of three daughters and stepmom to three through her marriage to Michael. After graduating from Queen's University and Ryerson's journalism program, Laura worked as an insurance adjuster, later becoming a communications coordinator/information and referral specialist in mental health. Her experience with loss led her to volunteer at Bereaved Families of Ontario/Halton-Peel, the Streetsville COPING program and Stephen Ministry. Laura credits a 19-year commitment to CBSI (Community Bible Study International) for helping her to keep the faith. She has been writing on and off since childhood, having been Editor of *Inter-Comm Community Newspaper* in Central Etobicoke at age 16. Her work has appeared in *The Toronto Star*, *The Toronto Sun*, *The Anglican*, and her church newspaper, *The Trinity Times*. If an issue stirs her, she will fire off a letter to the editor. Laura enjoys writing rhymes, essays, short stories and for children. *Special* is her first book.